THE BOOK OF
REGIONAL AMERICAN COOKING
SOUTHERN

THE BOOK OF
REGIONAL AMERICAN COOKING
SOUTHERN

Jeanette P. Egan

Photographed by
GLENN CORMIER

HPBooks

ANOTHER BEST-SELLING VOLUME FROM HPBooks

HPBooks
are published by The Berkley Publishing Group
200 Madison Avenue
New York, New York 10016

First HPBooks edition: November 1994

Published simultaneously in Canada.

Library of Congress Cataloguing-in-Publication Data

Egan, Jeanette P.
    The book of regional American cooking. Southern / Jeanette P.
Egan ; photographed by Glenn Cormier. — 1st HPBooks ed.
        p.   cm.
    Includes index.
    ISBN 1-55788-191-X
    1. Cookery, American—Southern style.   I. Title.
TX715.2.S68E33   1994
641.5975—dc20   94-17341
                                                                  CIP

PRINTED IN CHINA

10 9   8 7 6 5 4 3 2 1

This book is printed on acid-free paper.

Special thanks for props to Tom Vignapiano, Crate and Barrel, San Diego;
Annie Algar, The Pottery Shack, Laguna Beach; Anne Hakes, Williams-Sonoma,
San Diego; and Bohannons, San Diego.

CONTENTS

INTRODUCTION

In the South, eating and talking about food are favorite pastimes, and southern hospitality means offering food and drink to your guests, even if the last meal was only an hour ago. While eating one meal, the menu for the next one will be planned! And what menus they will be—platters of baked ham or fried chicken; rich, steaming homemade soups; bowls of fresh garden vegetables; hot, fragrant fresh-baked breads, spicy relishes, and luscious desserts. Even breakfasts do not escape the southern touch. They can feature baked grits, fried apples or fried corn, plates of sliced ripe tomatoes, and maybe even hot biscuits with southern sausage gravy, in addition to the bacon and eggs. Usually such feasts are now reserved for brunch on weekends or holidays featuring family get-togethers.

Food in the South has had many influences. The Native Americans taught the early English settlers about the use of corn, which is now one of the most important staples. Another important influence has been the cooking of the African Americans, who contributed many of the ingredients and the techniques of what is now called soul food. An entire new cuisine arose out of what were by necessity inexpensive and accessible foods.

The British colonists brought favorite recipes and adapted them to local ingredients. Some recipes for typical British dishes such as trifle are still almost exactly the same as in England. The British influence remains strong in the Appalachian region. Other early European influences were those of the French and Spanish. Some of the French were the Arcadians, the ancestors of the Cajuns. Later newcomers included the Germans and peoples of the Caribbean. The influence of the Caribbean continues to grow, and many markets feature the tropical fruits of that region.

Southern cooking has felt the impact of the interest in lower-fat, lower-calorie foods. The biggest change has been a reduced emphasis on animal fats for seasoning and cooking. Other recent changes have lightened some of the dishes and introduced new ingredients that have blended with the old. Many of the recipes included here reflect the new style of Southern eating.

Ingredients

Some of the ingredients grown in the South include pecans, peanuts, peaches, strawberries, and vegetables from commercial farms and family plots. Vegetable gardens are plentiful and produce a harvest of full-flavored vegetables. Because of the mild climate, it is possible to have both a summer garden and a cool-weather garden. Those who cannot have a garden do have at least a few pots of herbs or maybe a tomato growing among the flowers. Wild produce includes hickory nuts, black walnuts, blackberries, and mulberries.

Chickens and pigs are raised commercially in large barns and also in small farms for family use. Don't forget the contributions from the water—many of the South's favorite dishes feature fish or shellfish. Freshwater fish in local waters include bass, bluegills, crappie, bream, and catfish. Catfish, once available only from fishing, is now farmed. Farm-raised catfish has a cleaner, less musky flavor and is now widely available in supermarkets. Shrimp, oysters, crabs, crayfish, and both saltwater and freshwater fishes are available.

Beans

Beans, particularly dried beans, are important in the South. Pinto, red, white, and black beans are eaten. Most are available both canned and dried. If using canned beans, drain, rinse under running water, and drain again for a fresher flavor. Cooked dried beans can also be frozen.

Black-eyed peas

Called a pea although it is actually a bean, black-eyed peas are used in Hopping John and other dishes. They are available fresh, frozen, and canned. They are delicious as a side dish or added to salads.

Cornmeal

Most southerners prefer white cornmeal (and their cornbread unsweetened). Look for stone-ground cornmeal, it has a richer flavor. Keep stone-ground meal in the refrigerator or freezer, because it still contains the germ, which can become rancid at room temperature. Self-rising cornmeal is also available in bags for making cornbread.

Country Ham

Country ham differs from regular cured ham, because it is very salty and very low in moisture. It is aged for several months. Because of its rich, salty flavor, one ham will feed a crowd of people. Slice the cooked ham as needed very, very thinly. It will keep in the refrigerator for several weeks after cooking and can be used in small amounts in casseroles, sauces, and stuffing. It is the perfect meat to feature at a party where each person can slice off slivers of ham for nibbling.

Greens

Greens have always been popular in the South and now that everyone knows how good they are for us, their availability in supermarkets is increasing. They are more widely available in the cooler months. Common greens include collards, mustard, turnip, and dandelion greens. (Dandelion greens were once gathered from fields, but now commercially grown dandelion greens are available.)

Grits

Grits originally meant any finely ground grain but now generally refers to hominy grits. Once thought of as a food that only a southerner could love, grits are gaining wider acceptance and can be used in a variety of recipes from breads to main dishes.

Hominy

Hominy is made from dried corn that has been soaked in an alkaline solution to remove the skin and germ, washed, and then cooked until tender. It is available canned in supermarkets and moist and ready to cook in some markets (where it may be called *posole* and is purchased for use in a dish by the same name). The canned hominy is blander and softer than the freshly made product.

Nuts

Black walnuts have a pronounced flavor that is perfect for fudge, nut pies, and cakes. Hickory nuts have a richer flavor than

pecans and can be used in the same recipes. Unless you live in the South, black walnuts and hickory nuts are not widely available. Sometimes they are available by mail order. Pecans are grown throughout the South and are used in the justifiably famous southern pecan pie. Peanuts are not really nuts, they are legumes (like beans and peas) that grow underground. Peanuts and peanut butter are used in baked goods, soups, stews, and main dishes, and are eaten roasted and boiled as snacks.

Okra

The pod of a member of the hibiscus family, okra is available fresh, frozen, and pickled. Okra is used to add thickness and flavor to gumbos and is served as a vegetable side dish.

Soft-wheat Flour

Soft-wheat flour is low in protein (gluten) so it produces baked goods with a tender texture. It is particularly good for biscuits and cakes. Self-rising soft-wheat (and all-purpose) flour that has had baking powder and salt already added is widely available.

EQUIPMENT

In general, southern cooking can be done with standard cooking equipment. The only additions should be a cast-iron skillet for baking cornbread (and frying chicken) and a cast-iron cornstick pan for baking cornsticks. These, when heated before adding the batter, give the crusty crust that is typical of these breads.

Both skillets and cornstick pans (or any cast-iron pans) need to be seasoned by rubbing with vegetable shortening and heating in the oven on low before using. Wipe out any excess fat before using or storing. Skillets may need to be seasoned several times.

Well-seasoned cast-iron skillets become heirlooms and are passed down to family members. They become smooth and virtually nonstick with proper care. Clean quickly in hot water and mild soap, and do not soak or use harsh scrubbers. Dry thoroughly to prevent rusting and reseason as needed. Never, never put them in the dishwasher! Avoid steel skillets that look like cast-iron ones; they never season properly and food tends to stick to them when cooking. If you were not fortunate enough to inherit a good-quality iron skillet, check out garage sales for used ones.

Sweet Onion & Pepper Pie

2 tablespoons butter or margarine
1 tablespoon olive oil
3 large sweet onions, preferably Vidalia,
    thinly sliced crosswise
1 red bell pepper, roasted, peeled, and
    cut into thin strips
2 eggs, lightly beaten
1/2 cup half-and-half
1/2 teaspoon each salt and freshly
    ground pepper
Crust:
1 teaspoon active dried yeast
1/4 cup lukewarm water (110F, 45C)
2 cups all-purpose flour
1 tablespoon sugar
1 tablespoon baking powder
1/2 teaspoon salt
1/4 cup butter or margarine, softened
About 1/2 cup milk

Preheat oven to 400F (205C). Grease a 15" x
10" baking sheet. Heat butter and oil in a
large skillet over medium-low heat. Add
onions; cook, stirring occasionally, until softened, about 20 minutes. If onions brown,
reduce heat. Remove from heat; stir in bell
pepper. Combine eggs, half-and-half, salt, and
pepper in a small bowl.

Prepare Crust: Dissolve yeast in warm water.
Sift flour, sugar, baking powder, and salt into
a medium-size bowl. Stir in yeast mixture,
butter, and milk to make a moderately stiff
dough. Knead dough on a lightly floured
board until smooth.

Roll out dough to about a 16" x 11" rectangle.
Line prepared pan with dough. Cover with
plastic wrap. Let rise in a warm place about
15 minutes. Arrange onion mixture over
dough. Pour egg mixture over onions. Bake
about 20 minutes or until topping is set.
Cool slightly and cut into 20 pieces.

Makes 20 appetizers.

SAUSAGE-STUFFED POTATO SKINS

4 large baking potatoes
8 ounces spicy turkey or pork bulk
sausage
1 cup (4 oz.) shredded Monterey Jack
cheese
1/4 cup finely chopped green onions
with tops
1 tomato, seeded and chopped

Preheat oven to 375F (190C). Scrub potatoes. Bake potatoes 1 to 1-1/4 hours or until fork-tender. Cool until potatoes can be handled. Cook sausage in a medium-size skillet over medium heat until browned, stirring to break up sausage; drain well.

Cut potatoes in half lengthwise. Scoop out centers leaving about a 1/2-inch-thick shell. Reserve potato centers for another use. Preheat broiler.

Place potato shells on a baking sheet. Sprinkle sausage over potatoes. Top with cheese, onions, and tomato. Broil until cheese melts. Serve hot.

Makes 8 appetizers.

CRAB CAKES

1 pound crabmeat, picked over
1/4 cup diced onion
1/4 cup diced red bell pepper
3 cups fresh bread crumbs
1/2 cup mayonnaise
1/4 cup cream cheese, softened
1 tablespoon Dijon mustard
1 egg, lightly beaten
1/2 teaspoon dried leaf tarragon
1/8 teaspoon red (cayenne) pepper
1/8 teaspoon salt
2 tablespoons vegetable oil
Lemon wedges or slices to serve

Drain crabmeat well. Combine crabmeat, onion, bell pepper, and 1/2 cup of the crumbs in a medium-size bowl.

Beat mayonnaise, cream cheese, mustard, egg, tarragon, cayenne, and salt together in a medium-size bowl. Stir mayonnaise mixture into crabmeat mixture. Cover and refrigerate 30 minutes. Place remaining crumbs into a shallow bowl. Using an oval soup spoon, drop spoonfuls of mixture onto crumbs in batches. Coat cakes with crumbs.

Heat oil in a medium-size nonstick skillet over medium heat. Carefully add crab cakes; cook until golden brown, turning once. (If oil browns, wipe out skillet and add fresh oil.) Serve with lemon.

Makes about 24 appetizers.

Ham & Artichoke Pastries

1-1/2 cups all-purpose flour
1/2 cup butter or margarine, softened
1 (3-oz.) package cream cheese, softened
1 (14-oz.) jar marinated artichoke hearts
1 (7-oz.) jar roasted bell peppers,
   drained
8 ounces cooked ham, cut into small
   cubes
1 tablespoon chopped fresh thyme or 1
   teaspoon dried leaf thyme
1/2 teaspoon finely chopped fresh rosemary or 1/4 teaspoon dried rosemary

Combine flour, butter, and cream cheese in a medium-size bowl until mixture is a soft dough. Form into a ball; wrap in plastic wrap. Refrigerate 30 minutes or until chilled.

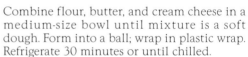

Preheat oven to 425F (220C). Cut any large artichoke hearts into quarters; drain well. Divide dough into 24 small balls. Press each ball into a small fluted pan or mini muffin cup, covering the bottom and part of the sides.

Arrange an artichoke piece in each pan or cup, and crisscross 2 strips of bell pepper over each artichoke. Top with some of the ham. Sprinkle with thyme and rosemary. Bake 8 to 10 minutes or until golden brown. Serve warm.

Makes about 24 appetizers.

CHEDDAR CHEESE CRACKERS

1 cup all-purpose flour
1/4 teaspoon dried leaf thyme
Dash of red (cayenne) pepper
2 cups (8 oz.) shredded sharp Cheddar
    cheese at room temperature
1/2 cup butter or margarine, softened
1 egg, lightly beaten
Sesame seeds, toasted
Poppy seeds
Grated Parmesan cheese

Combine flour, thyme, and cayenne in a medium-size bowl. Stir in Cheddar cheese and butter until mixture is a soft dough. Form into a ball; wrap in plastic wrap. Refrigerate 30 minutes or until chilled.

Preheat oven to 375F (190C). Cut dough in half. Roll out half of dough on a lightly floured surface until about 1/8 inch thick. Use a 1-inch cookie cutter to cut dough into rounds. (If dough becomes soft, refrigerate dough until firm.) Repeat with remaining dough.

Arrange rounds on ungreased baking sheets. Brush each round with egg. Sprinkle equal numbers of rounds with sesame seeds, poppy seeds, and Parmesan cheese. Bake about 8 minutes or until golden brown.

Makes about 140 crackers.

CRAB DIP

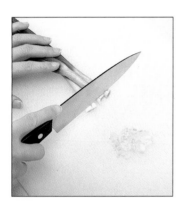

8 ounces crabmeat
1 bunch green onions with tops, finely
  chopped
1 small red bell pepper, finely chopped
1 large celery stalk, finely chopped
1-1/2 teaspoons chopped fresh tarragon
  or 1/2 teaspoon dried leaf tarragon
1/2 cup light sour cream
2 tablespoons mayonnaise
2 tablespoons fresh lemon juice or to
  taste
Hot pepper sauce to taste
Raw vegetables to serve

Drain crabmeat well. Pick out any bits of shell or cartilage, and flake crabmeat. Combine crabmeat, onions, bell pepper, celery, and tarragon in a medium-size bowl.

Stir in sour cream and mayonnaise. Season with lemon juice and hot pepper sauce. Cover and refrigerate 2 hours for flavors to blend. If dip is too thick, stir in a little milk. Spoon dip into a serving bowl. Serve with vegetables.

Makes about 2 cups.

DEVILED EGGS WITH HAM

12 eggs
3 tablespoons mayonnaise or plain
  yogurt
1-1/2 tablespoons Dijon mustard
2 teaspoons white-wine vinegar
3 tablespoons minced cooked ham or
  shrimp
2 tablespoons minced chives
White pepper to taste
Whole chives to garnish

Place eggs and enough water to cover in a
large saucepan. Bring to a boil, reduce heat,
cover, and simmer 15 minutes.

Immediately drain eggs and place in cold
water to cool. Remove shells. Cut eggs in half
lengthwise. Remove yolks and place in a
small bowl. Arrange whites on a plate. Mash
yolks with a fork and stir in mayonnaise,
mustard, and vinegar until smooth. Stir in
ham, chives, and pepper.

Spoon yolk mixture into a pastry bag fitted
with a large star tip. Pipe yolk mixture into
egg white halves. Serve immediately or
cover and refrigerate up to 8 hours. Garnish
with chives.

Makes 24 appetizers.

Variation
*To reduce the cholesterol per serving, discard half
of the cooked yolks. Stir in about 1/4 cup of any
pureed cooked vegetable.*

SHRIMP-STUFFED ARTICHOKES

3 tablespoons butter or margarine
1/4 cup all-purpose flour
2 cups chicken broth
2 teaspoons dried leaf tarragon or 1 teaspoon dried dill
White pepper
1/4 cup fresh lime juice
2 (13-3/4 -oz.) cans artichoke bottoms,
drained, rinsed
24 cooked, shelled medium-size shrimp
3/4 cup dried bread crumbs
1/4 cup freshly grated Parmesan cheese

Preheat oven to 400F (205C). Butter 12 heat-
proof dishes, each large enough to hold 1
artichoke bottom. Melt butter in a medium-
size saucepan. Stir in flour; cook, stirring,
until bubbly. Stir in broth; cook, stirring,
5 minutes.

Add tarragon, white pepper, and lime juice.
Arrange 1 artichoke bottom in each dish; top
each one with 2 shrimp.

Divide sauce among dishes. Sprinkle with
bread crumbs, then Parmesan cheese. Bake 15
minutes or until hot and bubbly.

Makes 12 servings.

CHICKEN WITH GUAVA SAUCE

3/4 cup guava nectar
1 tablespoon chopped fresh oregano
1 garlic clove, minced
1 tablespoon fresh lime juice
Freshly ground pepper
3 boneless skinless chicken breasts, cut
into 3/4 -inch strips
1 teaspoon cornstarch

Combine guava nectar, oregano, garlic, lime juice and pepper in a medium-size bowl.

Stir in chicken. Cover and refrigerate 1 hour. Preheat grill. Drain chicken, reserving marinade.

Thread chicken on skewers. Grill about 5 minutes, turning once. Meanwhile, whisk cornstarch into reserved marinade in a small saucepan. Cook over medium heat, whisking constantly, until slightly thickened and bubbly. Serve warm with kabobs.

Makes 12 appetizers.

Note
If using bamboo skewers, soak in water while the chicken is marinating.

HAM & HERBED BISCUITS

1 recipe Southern Biscuits (page 87)
1/2 teaspoon dried leaf thyme
About 8 ounces thin slices Baked
  Country Ham (page 62)
Mustard Butter:
1/4 cup butter or margarine, softened
2 tablespoons Dijon mustard
1 tablespoon minced chives

Prepare biscuits, adding thyme to dry ingredients. Use a 1-1/2 inch cookie cutter to cut biscuits. Bake as directed in recipe.

Prepare butter: Combine all ingredients in a small bowl.

Split biscuits. Spread one side with Mustard Butter. Top with ham. Serve warm.

Makes about 24 appetizers.

Variation
Honey mustard can be substituted for the Dijon mustard.

CATFISH FINGERS

3 catfish fillets (about 8 ounces each)
1 cup milk
Vegetable oil for deep-frying
1 cup corn flour or finely ground corn-
    meal
1/4 teaspoon dried leaf thyme, crushed
Salt and black pepper
Dash of red (cayenne) pepper
Tartar Sauce:
1 cup mayonnaise
2 tablespoons sweet pickle relish
2 tablespoons capers, chopped
Fresh lemon juice to taste

Cut catfish diagonally into 1-inch-wide strips.
Place into a medium-size bowl; add milk.
Turn to coat. Let stand 30 minutes.

Prepare sauce: Combine all ingredients in
a small bowl; cover and refrigerate until
needed.

Heat oil. Combine corn flour, thyme, salt,
black pepper, and cayenne in a shallow bowl.
Drain catfish. Dip pieces into flour mixture
to coat, shaking off extra coating. Fry in
batches until coating is golden brown and
fish is cooked. Drain on paper towels. Serve
with sauce.

Makes about 24 appetizers.

Note
*Lemon halves that have had the lemon segments
removed make excellent containers for individual servings of the Tartar Sauce.*

PICKLED OKRA ROLLS

16 pickled okra pods, drained
2 (3-oz.) packages light cream cheese,
softened
1 tablespoon Dijon mustard
8 slices cooked ham or smoked turkey
slices

Pat okra pods dry with paper towels. If desired, cut off the thin tips of the okra pods and discard. This makes the rolls more even for slicing.

Combine cream cheese and mustard in a small bowl. Spread ham slices with mustard mixture. Place an okra pod on the edge of each ham slice. Roll up jellyroll style.

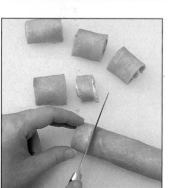

Place rolls on a plate. Cover with plastic wrap and refrigerate 30 minutes or up to 8 hours for the cream cheese to become firm. Cut each roll into 3 or 4 pieces. Serve with wooden picks.

Makes about 32 appetizers.

Variation
Substitute large dill pickle wedges or cooked fresh asparagus for the okra.

THREE-CHEESE SPREAD

8 ounces Cheddar cheese, shredded
  (2 cups)
4 ounces Monterey Jack cheese,
  shredded (1 cup)
1 (3-oz.) package cream cheese
1/4 cup beer
2 teaspoons Dijon mustard
2 garlic cloves, minced
1 teaspoon Worcestershire sauce
Hot pepper sauce to taste
Crackers and vegetables to serve

Bring all cheeses to room temperature.

Combine cheeses, beer, mustard, garlic,
Worcestershire sauce, and pepper sauce in a
food processor with the steel blade. Process
until smooth, stopping to scrape down side
of bowl one or two times.

Pack into a serving container. Cover and
refrigerate overnight to allow flavors to
blend. Bring to room temperature before
serving. Serve on crackers or use to stuff celery stalks, mushrooms, etc. This spread can
be prepared two or three days before serving.

Makes 2 cups.

Variation
*Spread on crackers and top each cracker with
fresh herbs or small pieces of vegetables such as
bell peppers.*

Easy Black Bean Soup

2 tablespoons olive oil
1 large onion, finely chopped
1 large garlic clove, minced
4 cups chicken broth
2 (15-oz.) cans black beans, drained
1/4 cup dry sherry (optional)
Sliced green onions to garnish

Heat oil in a medium-size saucepan. Add onion and garlic; cook, stirring occasionally, until softened.

Add broth and black beans. Simmer 5 minutes.

Process bean mixture in a food processor, in batches if necessary, until smooth. Return to saucepan, add sherry, if using, and heat until hot. Ladle into bowls. Garnish with green onions.

Makes 4 to 6 servings, about 7 cups.

Variations
Substitute almost any canned beans for the black beans. Tiny cooked sausage meatballs can be added after pureeing for a heartier soup.

Note
This is a light soup that is perfect as a first course.

WHITE BEAN SOUP

1 pound dried small white beans
5 cups water
5 cups chicken broth
1 large onion, chopped
1 large russet potato, chopped
1 large garlic clove, minced
2 bay leaves
2 flat-leaf parsley sprigs
Flat-leaf parsley leaves to garnish

Pick over beans, discarding broken beans and any rocks. Rinse beans. Soak overnight in water to cover. Drain beans.

Add soaked beans and water to a large pan. Boil 10 minutes. Reduce heat, cover, and simmer until beans are tender, about 1-1/2 hours. Add water as needed to keep beans covered.

When beans are tender, add broth, onion, potato, garlic, bay leaves, and parsley. Simmer, covered, until vegetables are tender. Discard bay leaves and parsley. Process about 1 cup of the soup in a food processor until pureed. Return puree to pan. Reheat if necessary. Spoon into bowls; garnish with parsley leaves.

Makes about 6 servings, 8 cups.

POTATO-SHRIMP-LEEK SOUP

2 large leeks
2 tablespoons butter or margarine
2 russet potatoes (about 1 pound),
  cubed
1 bay leaf
2 cups chicken broth
2 cups milk
1 tablespoon chopped fresh dill or 1 tea-
  spoon dried dill
Salt and white pepper
8 ounces small cooked, shelled shrimp
Dill sprigs to garnish

Cut green tops off leeks and discard. Make shallow lengthwise cuts in leeks and rinse under running water to remove all sand and dirt. Cut leeks crosswise into thin slices. Melt butter in a large saucepan. Add leeks; cook, stirring occasionally, until leeks are softened.

Add potatoes, bay leaf, and chicken broth to leeks. Simmer until potatoes are tender. Discard bay leaf. Process potato mixture in a food processor until pureed. Return to saucepan. Stir in milk, dill, salt, and pepper. Heat until hot; do not boil.

Stir in shrimp; heat until hot. Ladle into soup bowls. Garnish with dill sprigs.

Makes 4 servings, about 5 cups.

CRAB & CORN CHOWDER

2 tablespoons butter or margarine
1 large leek, white part only, chopped
2 celery stalks, chopped
1/2 red bell pepper, finely chopped
2 medium-size russet potatoes, diced
2 ears corn, kernels cut off and cobs
  scraped
3 cups chicken broth
1 teaspoon dried leaf thyme
8 ounces flaked crabmeat, picked over
2 tablespoons all-purpose flour mixed
  with 1/4 cup cold water
2 cups milk
Salt, freshly ground white pepper, and
  red (cayenne) pepper
About 2 tablespoons chopped flat-leaf
  parsley

Melt butter in a large saucepan over medium heat. Add leek, celery, and bell pepper; cook, stirring occasionally, until softened.

Add potatoes, corn, chicken broth, and thyme. Bring to a boil, reduce heat, cover and simmer about 20 minutes or until vegetables are tender.

Stir in crabmeat and the flour mixture; cook, stirring, until slightly thickened. Stir in milk; heat until hot without boiling. Season with salt, white pepper, and cayenne. Stir in parsley.

Makes 4 to 6 servings, about 7 cups.

VEGETABLE SOUP

1 tablespoon vegetable oil
2 celery stalks, thinly sliced crosswise
1 small white onion, chopped
4 medium-size tomatoes, chopped
1 large russet potato, unpeeled, cut into
    1/2-inch cubes
4 cups chicken broth or vegetable broth
1 cup fresh, frozen, or canned whole-
    kernel corn
1 cup sliced mushrooms
1 cup fresh or frozen green lima beans
1 bay leaf
1 thyme sprig or 1/2 teaspoon dried leaf
    thyme
1 oregano sprig or 1/2 teaspoon dried
    leaf oregano
1 small dried hot chile (optional)
Salt and freshly ground pepper
Parmesan cheese shavings to garnish

Heat oil in a large saucepan over medium-low heat. Add celery and onion; cook, stirring occasionally, until softened. Add tomatoes, potato, and broth. Bring to a boil, reduce heat, cover, and simmer about 10 minutes or until potato is almost tender.

Add corn, mushrooms, beans, herbs, and chile, if using. Simmer, covered, about 15 minutes or until all vegetables are tender. Discard herbs and chile. Season with salt and pepper. Ladle into bowls. Garnish with cheese.

Makes about 6 servings, about 8 cups.

JERUSALEM ARTICHOKE-ONION SOUP

1 pound Jerusalem artichokes, sliced
  crosswise
4 cups chicken broth
2 cups water
1 tablespoon butter or margarine
1 large onion, thinly sliced crosswise
1/4 teaspoon dried leaf thyme
Salt and white pepper
4 slices French-style bread
4 tablespoons freshly grated Parmesan
  cheese

Combine artichokes, chicken broth, and water in a large saucepan. Bring to a boil. Reduce heat, cover, and simmer until artichokes are tender. Meanwhile melt butter in a medium-size skillet over medium heat. Add onion and thyme; cook, stirring occasionally, until softened. Add onion and thyme to artichoke mixture. Bring to a boil, reduce heat, and simmer about 10 minutes to combine flavors. Season with salt and white pepper.

Preheat broiler. Arrange bread on a baking sheet; sprinkle each slice with 1 tablespoon cheese. Broil until browned. Ladle soup into 4 bowls. Place 1 bread slice over each serving.

Makes 4 servings, about 6 cups.

Note
Jerusalem artichokes, unrelated to globe artichokes, are sometimes called Sunchokes in supermarkets.

SHRIMP GUMBO

2 tablespoons vegetable oil
1 large onion, chopped
1 large garlic clove, minced
1 green bell pepper, chopped
1 red bell pepper, chopped
2 cups chopped fresh okra (about
   12 ounces)
1 pound plum tomatoes, chopped
4 cups chicken broth
1 small dried hot chile
1 bay leaf
1 pound medium-size shrimp, shelled
   and deveined
1/2 tablespoon chopped fresh oregano or
   1/2 teaspoon dried leaf oregano
1/2 tablespoon chopped fresh thyme or
   1/2 teaspoon dried leaf thyme
Salt and freshly ground black pepper
Steamed rice to serve

Heat oil in a Dutch oven over medium heat. Add onion; cook, stirring occasionally, until softened. Add bell peppers.

Add okra; cook, stirring occasionally, until okra no longer forms "strings." Add tomatoes, broth, chile, and bay leaf. Bring to a boil, reduce heat, cover and simmer until vegetables are tender, about 20 minutes.

Add shrimp, oregano, and thyme. Cook until shrimp turn pink, about 5 minutes. Season with salt and pepper. Discard bay leaf and chile. Serve gumbo over rice in bowls.

Makes 6 servings, 9 cups.

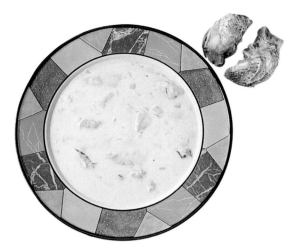

OYSTER STEW

2 tablespoons butter or margarine
2 tablespoons finely minced celery
1 tablespoon finely minced onion
2 tablespoons all-purpose flour
2 cups milk or 1 cup milk and 1 cup
half-and-half
1 pint fresh oysters
Salt and white pepper

Melt butter in a medium-size saucepan over medium heat. Add celery and onion; cook, stirring, until softened.

Stir in flour; cook, stirring, until bubbly. Stir in milk and oyster liquor. Cook, stirring occasionally, until mixture comes to a simmer.

Cut any large oysters in pieces. Add to stew. Cook until the edges of the oysters curl. Season with salt and pepper. Ladle into soup bowls.

Makes 2 servings, about 4 cups.

Variation
Oyster Bisque: Add 1/2 cup of hot milk mixture to 2 beaten egg yolks. Return to saucepan; simmer, stirring, until thickened, then add oysters.

TROPICAL CHICKEN SALAD

2 ripe mangoes
4 cups cooked rice
3 cups chopped cooked chicken
4 celery stalks, cut diagonally into thin
 slices
1 red bell pepper, finely chopped
1 jalapeño chile (optional), finely
 chopped
Orange Dressing:
¼ cup fresh orange juice
¼ cup extra-virgin olive oil
1 tablespoon white wine vinegar and
 ½ teaspoon dried leaf tarragon mixed
 together or 1 tablespoon tarragon
 vinegar
1 garlic clove, minced
1 teaspoon honey
Salt and freshly ground pepper

Peel mangoes. Cut flesh off seed into length-wise slices, then cut slices into ½-inch pieces.

Combine rice, chicken, mangoes, celery, red bell pepper, and chile, if using, in a medium-size bowl.

Prepare dressing: Whisk orange juice, olive oil, vinegar with tarragon, garlic, honey, salt, and pepper together until thickened. Pour dressing over salad and toss to combine.

Makes 4 servings.

HOMINY & BLACK BEAN SALAD

1 (14½-oz.) can white or yellow hominy
1 (15-oz.) can black beans
1 medium-size tomato, finely chopped
1 small onion, sliced into thin rings
¼ cup sliced pimento-stuffed olives,
   sliced into thin rounds
Chicory to garnish
Garlic-Cheese Dressing:
¼ cup extra-virgin olive oil
3 tablespoons sherry vinegar
1 garlic clove, minced
1 teaspoon sugar
Salt and freshly ground pepper
2 tablespoons freshly grated Parmesan
   cheese

Prepare dressing: Whisk together olive oil, vinegar, garlic, sugar, salt, and pepper. Whisk in cheese. Drain hominy and rinse with cold water. Drain well and place into a bowl. Drain beans and rinse with cold water. Drain well and place into bowl with beans.

Stir in tomato, onion, and olives. Toss with dressing; let stand at room temperature 30 minutes, tossing occasionally. Spoon salad onto salad plates; garnish with chicory.

Makes about 4 servings.

Wilted Greens Salad

4 slices lean hickory-smoked bacon
1 bunch green onions with tops, finely
   chopped
6 ounces tender dandelion greens,
   chopped
1 head leaf lettuce, separated into
   leaves, torn into bite-size pieces
   (about 10 oz.)
1 bunch spinach, stems removed and
   chopped
1/4 cup seasoned rice wine vinegar
2 hard-cooked eggs, finely chopped
Pear tomatoes to garnish (optional)

Cook bacon in a large skillet until crisp.
Remove with a slotted spoon and drain on
paper towels. Finely chop bacon; set aside.
Discard all except 1/4 cup drippings.

Add onions to hot drippings. Cook until
slightly softened. Add dandelion greens.
Cook, stirring, until wilted.

Add leaf lettuce and spinach. Toss in hot fat
until slightly wilted. Add vinegar and toss to
combine. Serve immediately, draining off
extra dressing. Sprinkle each serving with
bacon and hard-cooked eggs. Garnish with
tomatoes, if desired.

Makes 4 servings.

Variation
*Omit bacon. Heat 1/4 cup olive oil in skillet.
Continue as above.*

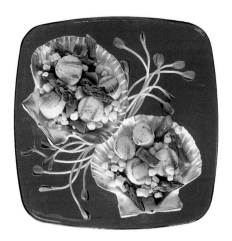

GRILLED SCALLOP SALAD

8 ounces sea scallops
2 ears corn
8 ounces fresh asparagus
Sunflower sprouts to garnish
Lime Vinaigrette:
1/4 cup extra-virgin olive oil
2 tablespoons fresh lime juice
1 tablespoon chopped fresh basil or
   1 teaspoon dried leaf basil
1 teaspoon sugar
Salt and freshly ground pepper

Preheat grill. Soak 4 wooden skewers in water. Rinse scallops and thread onto skewers. Pull back husks and remove silks from corn. Rinse under running water. Pull husks back into position.

Grill corn until milk is set, and grill scallops until opaque. Cool corn, remove husks, and cut off kernels. Steam asparagus over boiling water until crisp-tender. Cool asparagus in cold water; pat dry with paper towels. Prepare vinaigrette: Whisk together olive oil, lime juice, basil, sugar, salt, and pepper.

Toss corn kernels, asparagus, and scallops with a little of the vinaigrette. Spoon scallop mixture into serving dishes and drizzle with remaining vinaigrette. Garnish with sunflower sprouts.

Makes 2 main-dish or 4 first-course servings.

Note
For a first-course serving, arrange salad in clean scallop shells.

AMBROSIA

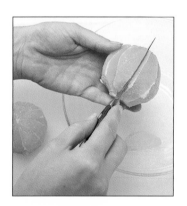

2 large oranges
1 large Red Delicious apple or Granny
**   Smith apple**
1/2 cup shredded coconut
Starfruit slices to garnish
Mint sprigs to garnish

Peel and segment oranges. If segments are
very large, cut them in half crosswise.

Squeeze remaining orange juice from mem-
branes into bowl. Cut apple in half and
remove core. Cut halves into thin wedges,
then cut wedges in half crosswise.

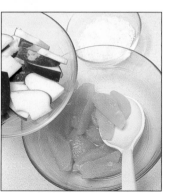

Toss apple with orange segments to coat with
orange juice. Add coconut and toss to combine. Cover and refrigerate until chilled.
Spoon ambrosia into serving dishes; garnish
with starfruit and mint.

Makes 4 servings.

Variations
Substitute fresh pineapple chunks or other fruit
for apple. Ambrosia always contains oranges and
coconut, but other fruits may vary. Toss salad
with 1 or 2 tablespoons of orange-flavored
liqueur, if desired.

PEPPERED COLE SLAW

1/2 large head green cabbage
1 green bell pepper
1 red bell pepper
Sour Cream Dressing:
3/4 cup regular or light sour cream
1/4 cup wine vinegar
1 tablespoon sugar
1/4 teaspoon salt
White pepper

Reserve some cabbage leaves for garnish, if desired. Shred remaining cabbage. Thinly slice bell peppers, cutting some strips for garnish, if desired. Toss shredded cabbage and bell pepper strips together in a medium-size bowl.

Prepare dressing: Combine sour cream, vinegar, sugar, salt, and pepper in a small bowl.

Pour dressing over cabbage mixture. Toss to combine. For a softer slaw, cover and refrigerate up to 4 hours. Garnish with bell pepper strips and cabbage leaves, if using.

Makes about 6 servings.

Variation
Add 1 teaspoon celery seeds to dressing.

BLACK-EYED PEA SALAD

2 (15-oz.) cans black-eyed peas
1 large tomato, chopped
2 large celery stalks, chopped
1/2 cup chopped green onions with tops
3 tablespoons extra-virgin olive oil
1 tablespoon white-wine vinegar
1 tablespoon shredded fresh basil or
**   1 teaspoon dried leaf basil**
Salt and freshly ground pepper
Basil leaves to garnish

Drain peas and rinse with cold water. Drain well. Place into a medium-size bowl.

Add tomato, celery, and green onions. Gently toss to combine.

Whisk together olive oil, vinegar, basil, salt, and pepper. Pour over salad; toss to combine. Let stand at room temperature 30 minutes, tossing occasionally, or refrigerate up to 8 hours. Garnish with basil leaves.

Makes 4 servings.

Variation
Substitute canned black beans or white beans for black-eyed peas.

TOMATO-CUCUMBER VINAIGRETTE

1/4 cup extra-virgin olive oil
1 tablespoon white-wine vinegar
1/2 tablespoon balsamic vinegar
2 teaspoons honey
Salt and freshly ground pepper
2 medium-size tomatoes, cut into wedges
1 cucumber, peeled in strips and cut
   into thin slices
1 tablespoon chopped fresh basil or 1
   teaspoon dried leaf basil
3 green onions with tops, thinly sliced
Butter lettuce leaves
Basil sprigs to garnish

Whisk together olive oil, vinegars, honey,
salt, and pepper in a small bowl.

Place cucumber and tomatoes in a medium-
size bowl. Add basil and green onions. Add
dressing and toss gently to combine. Cover
and refrigerate up to 1 hour, tossing occasionally. Arrange lettuce leaves on 4 salad
plates. Using a slotted spoon, arrange salad
on lettuce leaves. Garnish with basil sprigs.

Makes 4 to 6 servings.

SOFTSHELL CRAB SALAD

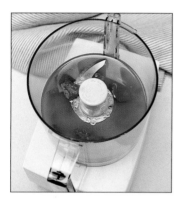

1/2 cup all-purpose flour
1/2 teaspoon dried leaf oregano
1/4 teaspoon red (cayenne) pepper
1/2 teaspoon salt
4 softshell crabs, ready to cook
2 tablespoons butter or margarine
2 tablespoons vegetable oil
4 cups mixed salad greens
Sun-dried Tomato Vinaigrette:
3 or 4 tablespoons fresh lemon juice
1 tablespoon seasoned rice wine vinegar
1/2 cup extra-virgin olive oil
4 sun-dried tomato halves, packed in oil,
   coarsely chopped
1 garlic clove, minced

Prepare vinaigrette: Combine all ingredients in a blender or small food processor. Process until slightly thickened.

Combine flour, oregano, cayenne, and salt in a shallow bowl. Coat crabs with flour mixture. Heat butter and oil in a large skillet over medium heat. Add coated crabs; sauté until browned, then turn and brown remaining sides.

Toss salad greens with vinaigrette. Arrange on 2 plates and top each salad with 2 cooked crabs.

Makes 2 main-dish salads.

Note
Seasoned rice wine vinegar is a mild rice wine vinegar seasoned with sugar and salt. It is available in the oriental food section of the supermarket and at specialty stores.

Vegetable-Pasta Salad

1 cup small broccoli flowerets
1 cup small cauliflowerets
1 carrot, sliced crosswise with a crinkle
  cutter
2 cups large pasta shells
1/2 cup ripe olives, halved lengthwise
1 celery stalk, thinly sliced crosswise
1 large tomato, chopped
1/2 cucumber, peeled in strips and
  sliced crosswise with a crinkle cutter
5 or 6 ounces feta cheese, cut into small
  cubes
1/4 cup extra-virgin olive oil
2 tablespoons white wine vinegar
2 tablespoons mayonnaise
1 teaspoon sugar
2 teaspoons finely chopped fresh basil
1 tablespoon finely chopped flat-leaf
  parsley
Salt and freshly ground pepper

Cook broccoli, cauliflower, and carrots separately in boiling water until crisp-tender. Drain and cool in iced water.

Cook pasta according to package directions until just tender to the bite. Drain, rinse with cold water, and drain well. Drain cooked vegetables; pat dry with paper towels. Toss together cooked vegetables, pasta, olives, celery, tomato, and cucumber in a large bowl. Add cheese and toss again.

Whisk together olive oil, vinegar, mayonnaise, sugar, herbs, salt, and pepper in a small bowl. Pour over salad and toss to combine. Serve immediately or cover and refrigerate up to 8 hours; toss again before serving.

Makes 6 servings.

CRAB-STUFFED SOLE

1 (14-oz.) can artichoke hearts, drained
and rinsed
1 tablespoon finely chopped green
onion
1 tablespoon chopped flat-leaf parsley
3 tablespoons seasoned dry bread
crumbs
8 ounces crabmeat, picked over and
flaked
4 (6-oz.) sole fillets
Salt and freshly ground pepper
Juice of 1/2 lime
Lime wedges to serve
Flat-leaf parsley to garnish

Preheat oven to 450F (220C). Butter 4 individual au gratin dishes or 1 large baking dish.
Process artichoke hearts in a food processor
until coarsely chopped.

Add onion, parsley, bread crumbs, and crabmeat. Process to combine. Set aside.

Arrange 1 sole fillet in each buttered dish.
Season with salt and pepper. Spoon artichoke mixture evenly over fillets, pressing
down slightly. Squeeze lime juice over stuffing. Bake 20 minutes or until topping is
brown and fish turns from translucent to
opaque. Serve with lime wedges and garnish
with parsley.

Makes 4 servings.

CRAB AU GRATIN

3 tablespoons butter or margarine
3 tablespoons all-purpose flour
1 cup milk
1 pound crabmeat, picked over and
   flaked
1 medium-size tomato, peeled, and
   finely chopped
2 tablespoons chopped flat-leaf parsley
2 tablespoons snipped chives
2 tablespoons dry sherry
Hot pepper sauce to taste
Salt and freshly ground pepper to taste
1/4 cup dried bread crumbs
1/4 cup freshly grated Parmesan cheese
Red pear tomatoes and flat-leaf parsley
   to garnish

Preheat oven to 400F (205C). Butter 1 large
oval baking dish or 4 individual au gratin
dishes. Melt butter in a medium-size
saucepan over medium heat. Stir in flour;
cook, stirring, until bubbly. Stir in milk;
cook, stirring, until thickened and floury
taste is gone.

Stir in crabmeat, tomato, parsley, chives,
sherry, hot pepper sauce, salt, and pepper.
Spoon mixture into buttered dishes.

Combine bread crumbs and cheese in a
small bowl. Sprinkle crumb mixture over
crabmeat mixture. Bake about 20 minutes
or until topping is browned and mixture
is bubbly.

Makes 4 servings.

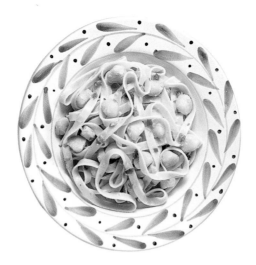

SCALLOPS WITH PASTA

2 tablespoons butter or margarine
2 shallots, finely chopped
1/2 green bell pepper, finely chopped
1/2 red bell pepper, finely chopped
1 pound sea or bay scallops
1 cup half-and-half
Salt and freshly ground pepper to taste
1 pound noodles, cooked according to
  package directions

Melt butter in a medium-size skillet over medium heat. Add shallots; cook until softened, stirring occasionally. Add bell peppers; cook until softened.

Rinse scallops. Cut large scallops in half. Add scallops to skillet; stir to combine. Add half-and-half. Cook until half-and-half is slightly reduced. Season with salt and pepper.

Drain noodles and place into a large bowl. Add scallop mixture and toss to combine.

Makes 4 servings.

FRIED OYSTERS

1 cup yellow cornmeal
1/4 cup all-purpose flour
1 teaspoon salt
1/2 teaspoon freshly ground pepper
Vegetable oil for frying
2 pints shucked oysters, drained
Tartar Sauce (page 23)
Lemon slices to garnish

Combine cornmeal, flour, salt, and pepper in a shallow bowl.

Heat 1 inch of oil in a medium-size skillet over medium heat. Pat oysters dry with paper towels. Coat with cornmeal mixture.

Fry in batches about 5 minutes or until golden, turning once. Drain on paper towels. Serve with Tartar Sauce. Garnish with lemon slices.

Makes 4 servings.

Variation
Use the fried oysters as a filling for poor boy sandwiches. Spread the tartar sauce inside the split buns and fill the buns with sliced tomatoes and onions, lettuce, and the oysters.

GARLIC SHRIMP WITH LEMON

2 tablespoons butter or margarine
1 tablespoon vegetable oil
1 small white onion, sliced lengthwise
1 green bell pepper, chopped
2 large garlic cloves, minced
1 pound shelled, deveined large shrimp
Salt and red (cayenne) pepper
Juice of 1/2 lemon
Steamed white rice to serve
Lemon slices and parsley to garnish

Heat butter and oil in a large skillet over medium heat. Add onion, bell pepper, and garlic; cook, stirring occasionally, until softened.

Add shrimp to skillet; cook, stirring occasionally, until shrimp are pink. Season with salt, cayenne, and lemon juice. Spoon shrimp and cooking juices over rice. Garnish with lemon slices and parsley.

Makes 4 servings.

Note
Do not overcook the shrimp or they will be tough.

BROILED CATFISH & SHRIMP

3 tablespoons olive oil
4 catfish fillets (about 4 oz. each)
1 small onion, finely chopped
1 small red bell pepper, finely chopped
1 teaspoon salt
Red (cayenne) pepper
1 lemon, thinly sliced
8 ounces medium-size shrimp, shelled,
    with tails on
2 tablespoons fresh lemon juice
Flat-leaf parsley to garnish

Preheat broiler. Pour 2 tablespoons of the oil into a baking dish large enough to hold catfish in one layer. Arrange fish in pan.

Sprinkle onion and bell pepper over fish. Sprinkle fish and vegetables with salt and cayenne.

Arrange lemon slices over fish. Broil 5 minutes. Toss shrimp with remaining oil and the lemon juice. Arrange shrimp around fish. Broil 5 to 7 minutes or until shrimp are pink and fish changes from translucent to opaque. Using a spatula, place fish and shrimp on 4 plates. Spoon cooking juices over fish. Garnish with parsley.

Makes 4 servings.

SNAPPER CREOLE

2 tablespoons vegetable oil
1 medium-size onion, chopped
1 large garlic clove, minced
1 large green bell pepper, chopped
2 celery stalks, thinly sliced crosswise
1 (1-lb.) can tomatoes
1 bay leaf
Salt and freshly ground pepper
1-1/2 pounds red snapper fillets
Steamed rice to serve
Flat-leaf parsley to garnish

Heat oil in a medium-size saucepan over medium heat. Add onion and garlic; cook until softened.

Add bell pepper, celery, tomatoes with juice, and bay leaf. Cook, stirring occasionally, 30 minutes. Season with salt and pepper.

Preheat oven to 400F (205C). Grease a 13" x 9" baking pan. Rinse fish and arrange in prepared pan. Pour sauce over fish. Bake about 20 minutes, depending on thickness of fish, or until fish turns from translucent to opaque. Spoon rice onto serving plates. Using a spatula, place fish on plates; spoon sauce over fish. Garnish with parsley.

Makes 4 servings.

CHICKEN LIVERS ON TOAST

2 tablespoons olive oil
4 green onions, cut into 1-inch lengths
1 red bell pepper, cut into 1-inch
   squares
1 garlic clove, minced
8 ounces chicken livers
1 teaspoon finely chopped fresh sage or
   1/4 teaspoon dried leaf sage
Salt and freshly ground pepper
French bread slices, toasted
Sage sprigs to garnish

Heat oil in a medium-size skillet over medium heat. Add onions, bell pepper, and garlic; cook until softened. Remove with a slotted spoon.

Add chicken livers to skillet; cook until browned on the outside and almost cooked through. Season with sage, salt, and pepper.

Return vegetables to skillet; cook, stirring, until livers are cooked through. Serve hot on toast. Garnish with sage sprigs.

Makes 2 or 3 servings.

ORANGE-GLAZED GRILLED CHICKEN

1 (3-lb.) broiler-fryer chicken, cut into serving pieces
Salt and freshly ground pepper
Orange Glaze:
1/2 cup fresh orange juice
1/4 cup honey
1/4 cup butter or margarine, melted
2 tablespoons grated orange peel

Preheat grill. Prepare glaze: Bring orange juice, honey, butter, and orange peel to a boil in a small saucepan.

Season chicken with salt and pepper. Grill chicken over hot coals until browned on one side. Turn and grill remaining side until chicken is browned, about 20 minutes total.

Brush chicken with glaze, turning and brushing other side. Grill until juices run clear when chicken is pierced with a fork, about 10 minutes total. Serve hot.

Makes 4 servings.

CHICKEN & HERB DUMPLINGS

1 (3-1/2 lb.) stewing chicken
2 tablespoons vegetable oil
1 large onion, cut into wedges
2 carrots, cut crosswise into 1-inch
  pieces
1 celery stalk, cut crosswise into 1-inch
  pieces
6 cups chicken broth
Herbed Dumplings:
1-1/2 cups all-purpose flour
1-1/2 teaspoons baking powder
1 teaspoon salt
1 teaspoon dried leaf thyme
1/4 cup butter or margarine, chilled
3/4 cup milk

Cut chicken into serving pieces, removing as much of the fat and skin as possible. Heat oil in a Dutch oven. Add chicken and cook until browned, turning occasionally.

Remove chicken. Add vegetables to pan. Cook over low heat until vegetables are softened. Add stock and chicken. Simmer, covered, until chicken is tender, about 35 minutes.

Prepare dumplings: Sift flour, baking powder, and salt into a medium-size bowl. Stir in thyme. Cut in butter until mixture resembles coarse crumbs. Stir in milk to make a stiff batter. Drop batter by spoonfuls onto simmering chicken mixture. Cover and cook 20 minutes without opening lid.

Makes 6 to 8 servings.

CHICKEN HASH

2 tablespoons olive oil
1/2 cup chopped onion
1/2 each red and green bell pepper,
  chopped
4 ounces fresh mushrooms, chopped
3 tablespoons all-purpose flour
1 cup chicken broth
1/2 cup milk
2 cups chopped cooked chicken
2 tablespoons dry sherry
Salt and freshly ground black pepper
Cornbread, biscuits, or cooked rice to
  serve

Heat olive oil in a large skillet over medium heat. Add onion; cook until softened. Add bell peppers and mushrooms. Cook until bell peppers are softened and onion is done.

Stir in flour. Stir in chicken broth and milk. Cook, stirring, until mixture is bubbly and thickened.

Stir in chicken and sherry. Season with salt and black pepper; cook, stirring, until heated through. Cut squares of cornbread in half; arrange on plates. Spoon hash over cornbread.

Makes about 4 servings.

SPRINGTIME POT PIES

8 ounces pearl onions
12 ounces asparagus spears, trimmed,
    cut in 1-inch pieces
8 ounces mushrooms, quartered
3 cups cooked chicken or turkey, cut in
    1-inch cubes
3 tablespoons butter or margarine
3 tablespoons all-purpose flour
2 cups white wine or chicken broth
Salt and freshly ground pepper to taste
1/4 cup chopped flat-leaf parsley
1 tablespoon fresh thyme or 1 teaspoon
    dried leaf thyme
1 teaspoon ground coriander
1 (17-1/4-oz.) 1/4 package frozen puff
    pastry, thawed
Thyme sprigs to garnish

Preheat oven to 400F (205C). Blanch onions
in boiling water 3 minutes; cool immediately
in cold water, then peel. Blanch asparagus in
boiling water 2 minutes; cool immediately in
cold water.

Combine asparagus, onions, mushrooms,
and chicken in a medium-size bowl. Spoon
equal amounts into 4 (1-1/2-cup) ovenproof
baking dishes; set aside. Melt butter in a
medium-size saucepan. Add flour; cook, stirring, until foamy. Gradually stir in wine.
Cook, stirring, until bubbly and thickened.
Season with salt and pepper. Stir in parsley,
thyme, and coriander. Pour equal amounts of
sauce over contents of each dish; set aside.

On a lightly floured surface, roll out half of
pastry to a rectangle about 14" x 10". Cut out
2 rounds about 1 inch larger than top of
dish. Repeat with remaining pastry. Place a
pastry round over filling in each dish. Use
pastry scraps to decorate pastry, if desired.
Place dishes on baking sheets. Bake 20 minutes, until pastry is puffed and golden brown.

Makes 4 servings.

BAKED CHICKEN & PLANTAINS

3 tablespoons mango chutney, such as
   Major Grey's
1 teaspoon green peppercorns, drained,
   rinsed
1 teaspoon Dijon mustard
1/2 cup fresh orange juice
4 boneless skinless chicken breast halves
2 ripe plantains
1/2 papaya, sliced lengthwise
Cilantro sprigs to garnish

In a blender or food processor, combine chutney, peppercorns, mustard, and orange juice.
Process until smooth. Rinse chicken with
cold water; pat dry with paper towels. Place
chicken in a glass or stainless steel bowl. Pour
chutney mixture over chicken. Let marinate 1
hour at room temperature.

Preheat oven to 425F (220C). Grease a baking
dish large enough to hold chicken in one
layer. Peel plantain; cut crosswise in 1/4-inch
slices. Arrange plantains in greased dish.
Arrange chicken over plantains, adding all of
marinade. Cover and bake about 25 minutes
or until chicken is cooked through and plantains are tender.

Remove from oven; preheat broiler. Arrange
papaya around chicken. Baste papaya and
chicken with cooking juices. Broil until
chicken is brown and papaya is warm. Divide
among 4 plates. Garnish with cilantro sprigs.

Makes 4 servings.

GRILLED WHOLE CHICKEN

1 (3-lb.) chicken
4 to 6 bay leaves
Fresh thyme sprigs
6 garlic cloves, sliced into thin pieces
Salt and freshly ground pepper to taste

Prepare covered grill for indirect cooking.
Rinse chicken; reserve giblets for other uses.
Season chicken with salt and pepper.

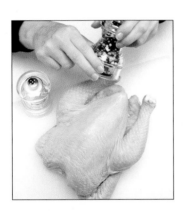

Loosen skin over breast and back by insert-
ing finger gently under skin. After skin is
loose, insert half the bay leaves, thyme, and
garlic under skin.

Place remaining bay leaves, thyme, and garlic
in chicken cavity. Tie legs together with
kitchen string, if desired. Place over hot coals,
cover grill, and cook until chicken is
browned and juices run clear when chicken
is pierced with a knife, about 1 hour.

Makes 4 servings.

Variation
*Preheat oven to 375F (190C). Place chicken on a
rack in a baking pan. Bake about 1-1/4 hours or
until juices run clear when chicken is pierced
with a knife.*

FRIED CHICKEN

1 (2-1/2- to 3-lb.) broiler-fryer chicken,
  cut into serving pieces
About 1 cup buttermilk or milk
1-1/2 cups all-purpose flour
1 teaspoon salt
1 teaspoon black pepper
Dash of red (cayenne) pepper
1 teaspoon dried leaf thyme
1/4 teaspoon ground sage
Vegetable oil for frying
Milk Gravy:
3 tablespoons all-purpose flour
2 cups milk
Salt and freshly ground pepper to taste

Arrange chicken in a large pan. Pour butter-milk over chicken; let stand at room temperature about 30 minutes.

Combine flour, salt, black pepper, cayenne, thyme, and sage in a plastic bag. Drain chicken, shaking off excess milk. Shake chicken in flour mixture, a few pieces at a time. Arrange on a wire rack to dry while oil heats.

Heat about 2 inches of oil in a large skillet to 350F (175C). Add chicken, starting with the dark meat, a few pieces at a time to keep the temperature up. Cook until golden brown. Cover skillet and cook until chicken juices run clear when chicken is pierced with a knife, 20 to 30 minutes.

Remove chicken from skillet; drain on paper towels. Keep warm in a 250F (120C) oven.

Prepare gravy: Drain fat from skillet, leaving about 2 tablespoons of oil. Stir in flour, scraping up any browned bits from skillet. Cook, stirring, until bubbly.

Stir in milk. Cook, stirring, until mixture is thickened. Season with salt and pepper. Serve gravy over mashed potatoes or hot biscuits.

Makes about 4 servings.

FRIED CHICKEN IN BATTER

1 (2-1/2- to 3-lb.) broiler-fryer chicken,
  cut into serving pieces
Vegetable oil for frying
Batter:
1 cup all-purpose flour
About 1 cup milk
1 egg
1/2 teaspoon salt
1/2 teaspoon black pepper
Dash of red (cayenne) pepper

Prepare batter: Combine flour, 1 cup milk, egg, salt, black pepper, and cayenne in a blender or food processor. Process until combined. Cover and refrigerate 1 hour. Stir in more milk, if needed. Batter should be about the consistency of heavy cream. Pour batter into a bowl.

Heat about 2 inches of oil in a large skillet to 350F (175C). Dip chicken into batter to coat. Drain off excess batter.

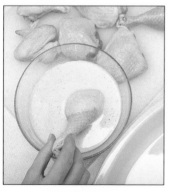

Add chicken, starting with the dark meat, a few pieces at a time to keep the temperature up. Cook until golden brown. Cover skillet and cook until chicken juices run clear when chicken is pierced with a knife, 20 to 30 minutes.

Makes about 4 servings.

Variation
If everyone prefers mostly dark or light meat, substitute chicken parts for a whole chicken.

Stuffed Turkey Breast

1 (4-lb.) turkey breast
Salt and freshly ground pepper
Sausage-Cornbread Stuffing:
1/2 pound turkey sausage
1 small onion, chopped
1 celery stalk, chopped
1 cup whole-kernel corn
1/2 cup crumbled cornbread
1/2 cup dried bread cubes
1 teaspoon dried leaf sage
1/2 teaspoon dried leaf basil
1/4 teaspoon dried leaf oregano
Salt and freshly ground pepper
About 1/2 cup chicken broth

Preheat oven to 350F (175C). Prepare stuffing: Cook sausage in a large skillet until no longer pink, breaking up meat. Add onion and celery; cook until softened. Remove from heat. Stir in corn, cornbread, bread cubes, herbs, salt, and pepper. Stir in just enough broth to moisten dressing; let cool.

Remove bones from turkey: First, cut around ribs until they are free on both sides. Then cut around breast bone, scraping meat from bone alternately with knife and fingers. Finally cut through the cartilage to release the bone.

Spread turkey breast, skin-side down, on a flat surface. Spread dressing over turkey. Starting at one long side, roll up turkey, enclosing stuffing. Tie with kitchen string. Place seam side down in a roasting pan. Cook 1-1/4 to 1-1/2 hours or until juices run clear when turkey is pierced with a knife or a meat thermometer registers 170F (76C). Let stand about 10 minutes before slicing. Serve hot.

Makes 6 to 8 servings.

BAKED COUNTRY HAM

1 (about 15-lb.) cured ham
Honey-Mustard Glaze:
1/3 cup light brown sugar
1/3 cup honey
2 tablespoons Dijon mustard
2 tablespoons dry sherry

Scrub any mold from ham with a stiff brush in a sink under running water. Soak ham in cold water to cover 24 hours, changing water at least once. Drain and discard water. Preheat oven to 350F (175C). Place ham in a large roaster and cover with water. Bake about 2 hours. Drain and discard water. Turn ham and add hot water to cover. Bake about 2-1/2 hours or until a meat thermometer registers 170F (75C).

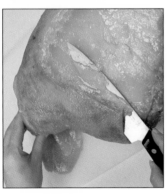

Let ham cool in cooking water. Drain ham. Cut off ham skin and most of the fat. Preheat oven to 375F (190C). Prepare glaze: Combine all ingredients in a small bowl.

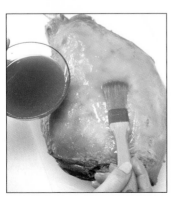

Brush ham with glaze. Place ham in a roasting pan. Bake about 30 minutes or until ham is glazed. Let rest 30 minutes. Cut into very thin slices to serve. The baked ham, tightly covered, will keep several weeks in the refrigerator.

Makes about 30 servings.

Note
Country hams are often covered with mold when purchased. This does not mean that the ham has spoiled. Simply brush away the mold under cold running water. The soaking is necessary to remove some of the salt and rehydrate the ham.

PORK CHOPS WITH RICE

2 tablespoons olive oil
4 pork chops
1/4 cup finely chopped onion
1/2 cup finely chopped orange bell
   pepper
1 cup long-grain white rice
1 large tomato, chopped
1 bunch collard greens, large stems
   removed, finely shredded
2 cups chicken broth
1 teaspoon minced dried rosemary
Salt and freshly ground pepper
Rosemary sprigs to garnish

Preheat oven to 350F (175C). Heat oil in a Dutch oven over medium heat. Add pork chops; brown on both sides. Remove pork chops from pan.

Add onion and bell pepper to pan; cook until softened. Stir in rice; cook, stirring, until rice is coated with oil. Stir in tomato and collard greens.

Add chicken broth, rosemary, salt, and pepper. Arrange pork chops over rice. Cover and bake 30 minutes. Remove lid and bake until liquid evaporates and rice is tender, about 20 minutes. Spoon rice onto dinner plates; top each serving with a pork chop. Garnish with rosemary.

Makes 4 servings.

STUFFED PORK TENDERLOIN

2 pork tenderloins (about 1-1/2 lbs. total)
Herbed Dressing:
1 small onion, chopped
1 celery stalk, chopped
2 cups crumbled cornbread
1 cup chopped green chiles (about 6
   roasted chiles)
1/2 red bell pepper, chopped
1 garlic clove, minced
1 teaspoon dried leaf thyme
1/2 teaspoon dried leaf basil
Salt and freshly ground black pepper

Preheat oven to 350F (175C). Prepare stuffing: Cook onion and celery until softened. Combine cooked vegetables, cornbread, chiles, bell pepper, garlic, herbs, salt, and black pepper in a medium-size bowl.

Lightly grease a 13" x 9" baking pan. Cut tenderloins lengthwise almost all the way through. Pound to a uniform thickness of about 1/2 inch.

Place one tenderloin on work surface; lap remaining tenderloin over end of the first one. Top tenderloins with stuffing, pressing down lightly. Roll up jellyroll style, starting at one long side. Tie with kitchen string. Place in a baking pan. Bake about 1 hour or until browned on top and a meat thermometer registers 170F (75C). Let stand 15 minutes before slicing.

Makes about 6 servings.

PORK ROAST WITH ONIONS

1 cup finely chopped white onion
1 garlic clove, minced
1 tablespoon chopped parsley
1 tablespoon fresh thyme or 1 teaspoon
   dried leaf thyme
1/2 teaspoon salt
1/4 teaspoon red (cayenne) pepper or
   to taste
Freshly ground black pepper
1 (3-lb.) rolled boneless pork loin roast
3/4 cup white wine or sherry mixed
   with 1-1/2 tablespoons cornstarch

Preheat oven to 400F (205C). Combine onion,
garlic, parsley, thyme, salt, cayenne, and black
pepper in a small bowl.

Untie roast. Place 1/4 of onion mixture on a
foil sheet large enough to enclose roast. Place
bottom half of roast on onion mixture.
Arrange 1/2 of onion mixture on meat; top
with remaining half. Spread remaining onion
mixture over top of roast. Seal tightly in foil.

Roast 1 hour. Uncover and roast 30 minutes
or until a meat thermometer registers 170F
(75C) and roast is browned. Place roast on a
serving platter. Cut into slices to serve. Pour
cooking juices into a small saucepan; stir in
wine mixture. Cook over medium heat until
slightly thickened. Spoon sauce over roast.

Makes 6 to 8 servings.

PORK WITH PEPPERCORN SAUCE

1 (about 1-lb.) pork tenderloin
1/2 cup all-purpose flour
1/2 teaspoon ground sage
Salt and freshly ground pepper
2 tablespoons olive oil
1 garlic clove, minced
Peppercorn Sauce:
1/2 cup white wine mixed with 1 tea-
    spoon cornstarch
2 tablespoons light sour cream
1 tablespoon minced chives
1 tablespoon green peppercorns,
    coarsely chopped

Cut pork diagonally across the grain into 1/2-inch-thick slices. Pound to 1/4-inch thickness.

Combine flour, sage, salt, and pepper in a shallow bowl. Lightly flour pork, shaking off excess flour. Heat oil in a large skillet. Add pork and garlic; cook until lightly browned, turning once.

Remove pork from skillet; keep warm. Add wine mixture to skillet. Cook, stirring, until thickened. Stir in sour cream, chives, and peppercorns. Heat until hot, stirring; do not boil. Serve sauce over pork.

Makes 3 or 4 servings.

BEEF & VEGETABLE STEW

1-1/2 pounds lean beef round steak, cut
   into 1-inch pieces
1/2 cup all-purpose flour seasoned with
   salt and pepper
2 tablespoons vegetable oil
3 cups beef broth
3 cups water
2 large carrots, cut into 1-inch rounds
1 large onion, cut into 1/2-inch wedges
2 large red potatoes, cut into 1-inch
   cubes
2 chayotes, cut into 1-inch pieces
2 ears corn, cut into 1-inch rounds
1 bay leaf
1 teaspoon dried leaf thyme
Salt and freshly ground pepper
Chopped chives to garnish

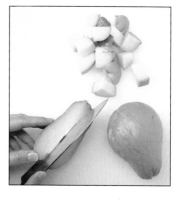

Shake beef with seasoned flour in a large bag
until coated. Heat oil in a nonstick Dutch
oven over medium heat. Add beef in batches;
cook, stirring occasionally, until browned.
Add broth and water; bring to a boil, reduce
heat, cover, and simmer 45 minutes.

Add carrots, onion, potatoes, chayotes,
corn, herbs, salt, and pepper. Simmer, covered, about 30 minutes or until meat and
vegetables are tender, stirring occasionally.
Discard bay leaf. Ladle into bowls. Sprinkle
with chives.

Makes about 6 servings.

STEAK WITH BOURBON SAUCE

1/2 cup bourbon
1/4 cup reduced-sodium soy sauce
2 tablespoons olive oil
3 green onions with tops, finely
  chopped
2 garlic cloves, minced
1 (3-lb.) beef round steak
Freshly ground pepper
1/4 cup Dijon mustard
1 cup half-and-half

Combine bourbon, soy sauce, oil, green onions, and garlic in a small bowl. Place steak in a plastic bag; pour bourbon mixture over steak. Seal bag and marinate at room temperature 1 hour.

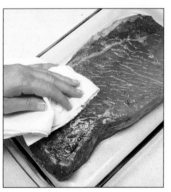

Preheat grill. Remove steak from marinade, reserving marinade, and pat dry. Sprinkle with pepper. Grill steak to desired doneness.

Pour reserved marinade into a small saucepan; boil until reduced by half. Stir in mustard and half-and-half. Cook, stirring, until slightly thickened. Thinly slice steak on the diagonal. Serve with mustard sauce.

Makes about 6 servings.

Note
No additional salt is needed because of the salt in the soy sauce and mustard.

CURRIED BEEF POT PIES

8 ounces pearl onions
12 ounces cauliflowerets
8 ounces mushrooms, quartered
1/2 large red bell pepper, cut in strips
  lengthwise
3 cups cooked cubed beef
3 tablespoons butter
3 tablespoons all-purpose flour
2 cups beer
Salt and freshly ground pepper
1 teaspoon curry powder
1/2 recipe Southern Biscuit dough
  (page 87)
1 egg white, lightly beaten
1 tablespoon sesame seeds

Preheat oven to 400F (205C). Blanch onions in boiling water 3 minutes; cool immediately in cold water, then peel. Blanch cauliflowerets in boiling water 1 minute; cool immediately in cold water. Combine cauliflowerets, onions, mushrooms, bell pepper, and beef in a medium-size bowl.

Spoon equal amounts into 4 (1-1/2-cup) ovenproof bowls; set aside. Melt butter in a medium-size saucepan. Add flour; cook, stirring, until foamy. Gradually stir in beer. Cook, stirring, until bubbly and thickened. Season with salt and pepper. Stir in curry powder. Pour equal amounts of sauce over contents of each bowl; set aside.

On a lightly floured surface, roll out dough to about 1/2-inch thickness. Cut out rounds about 1 inch smaller than top of bowl. Top bowls with pastry rounds. Brush rounds with egg white, then sprinkle with sesame seeds. Place bowls on baking sheets. Bake 20 minutes, until biscuits are puffed and golden brown.

Makes 4 servings.

BARBECUED BEEF BRISKET

1 (4- to 5-lb.) beef brisket
1 bay leaf
1 dried hot red chile
1 teaspoon peppercorns
1/2 lemon, thinly sliced
Barbecue Sauce:
1 tablespoon olive oil
1 large onion, chopped
2 garlic cloves, minced
1 (15-oz.) can tomato sauce
3 cups ketchup
1/2 cup cider vinegar
1/3 cup honey
1-1/2 tablespoons Dijon mustard
1 tablespoon chili powder
Hot pepper sauce to taste

Put beef in a large pan. Add bay leaf, chile, peppercorns, and lemon. Add enough water to cover. Simmer, covered, until beef is tender, about 2-1/2 hours, adding water as needed.

Prepare sauce: Heat oil in a large saucepan. Add onion and garlic; cook, stirring occasionally, until softened. Add remaining sauce ingredients. Simmer about 20 minutes.

Drain meat, discarding cooking liquid. Preheat grill. Grill meat until browned, turning once. Brush with sauce and cook a few more minutes. Slice meat thinly on the diagonal and serve with additional sauce.

Makes 6 servings.

RED BEANS & RICE

1 pound dried red kidney beans
6 cups water
1 ham hock (optional)
1 onion, chopped
1 green bell pepper, finely chopped
1 celery stalk, thinly sliced
1 garlic clove, minced
1 small dried hot chile (optional)
Salt and freshly ground pepper
Steamed rice to serve

Pick over beans, discarding broken beans and any rocks. Rinse beans. Soak overnight in water to cover. Drain beans.

Add beans, water, and ham hock, if using, to a large pan. Boil 10 minutes. Reduce heat, cover, and simmer until beans are tender, about 1-1/2 hours. Add water as needed to keep beans covered.

Add onion, bell pepper, celery, garlic, and chile, if using, to beans. Simmer until vegetables are tender. Season with salt and pepper. Remove ham hock if used, cool slightly, and cut meat into small pieces. Return meat to beans. Serve beans in bowls over rice.

Makes 4 to 6 servings.

SOUP BEANS

1 pound dried pinto beans
6 cups water
1 bay leaf
1 ham hock (optional)
Salt and freshly ground pepper
Chopped onion and chopped tomato to
serve
Buttermilk Cornsticks (page 90) to serve

Pick over beans, discarding broken beans and any rocks. Rinse beans. Add enough water to cover by 2 inches and soak beans overnight. Drain beans.

Add beans, water, bay leaf and ham hock, if using, to a large pan. Boil 10 minutes. Reduce heat, cover and simmer until tender, about 1-1/2 hours. Add water as needed; beans should be "soupy."

Discard bay leaf. Season with salt and pepper. Serve in bowls. Top with onion and tomato. Serve with cornsticks.

Makes 4 to 6 servings.

Note
These are called soup beans because they are served with lots of the cooking liquid, almost like a soup. Some people like to dunk cornbread in the liquid.

OKRA, CORN, & TOMATOES

1 tablespoon butter or margarine
1 tablespoon vegetable oil
12 ounces fresh okra, cut into thin
    rounds
2 ears corn, kernels cut off
2 medium-size tomatoes, chopped
Salt and freshly ground pepper

Heat butter and oil in a medium-size sauce-pan. Add okra; cook, stirring occasionally, until okra no longer forms "strings."

Stir in corn and tomatoes. Simmer, covered, over low heat until vegetables are tender, stirring occasionally. Season with salt and pepper.

Makes 4 to 6 servings.

Variation
If fresh okra isn't available, substitute sliced frozen okra.

HERBED GRITS SOUFFLÉ

4 cups water
1 cup grits
1 teaspoon salt
2 green onions with tops, finely
**   chopped**
2 garlic cloves, minced
1 tablespoon chopped mixed fresh herbs
**   or 1 teaspoon dried leaf herbs**
1 cup (4 oz.) shredded Cheddar cheese
3 eggs, separated
Freshly ground pepper

Preheat oven to 400F (205C). Grease 6 (1-cup) soufflé dishes. Bring water, grits, and salt to a boil in a medium-size saucepan. Cook, stirring, until thickened.

Remove from heat. Beat in onions, garlic, herbs, cheese, egg yolks, and pepper.

Beat egg whites in a medium-size bowl until stiff but not dry. Fold into grits mixture. Pour into prepared dishes. Bake about 25 minutes or until puffed and browned. Serve immediately.

Makes 6 servings.

Variation
Bake in a 1-1/2-quart greased baking dish in a 375F (190C) oven for about 40 minutes.

RUTABAGAS & POTATOES

**2 pounds rutabagas, cut into 1-inch
  cubes
1-1/4 pounds russet potatoes, cut into
  1-inch cubes
Salt
About 1/4 cup milk
2 tablespoons butter or margarine
1/8 teaspoon freshly grated nutmeg
Salt and freshly ground white pepper
Parsley sprigs to garnish**

Cook rutabagas and potatoes in separate
saucepans in boiling salted water until tender, 20 to 30 minutes.

Drain rutabagas and potatoes. Combine in a
large bowl and mash.

Beat in milk, butter, nutmeg, salt, and pepper. Spoon into a serving bowl. Garnish with
parsley sprigs. Serve hot. This dish is particularly good with pork dishes.

Makes about 6 servings.

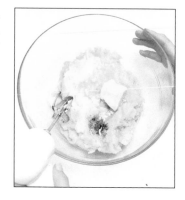

CONFETTI CORN WITH BACON

2 ears corn
2 hickory-smoked lean bacon slices,
  diced
1/4 cup finely chopped white onion
1/2 green bell pepper, chopped
1/2 red bell pepper, chopped
Salt and freshly ground pepper
Milk, if needed

Cut corn from cobs, then scrape cobs with
the back of a knife; set aside.

Cook bacon in a medium-size skillet over
medium heat until crisp. Add onion and bell
peppers; cook until onion is softened.

Add corn; cover and cook, stirring occasionally, over low heat until corn is tender, about
15 minutes. Add a little milk if corn becomes
too dry.

Makes 4 servings.

Variation
Bacon can be omitted. Add 1 tablespoon olive oil
to skillet before adding onion and bell peppers.

POTATOES & SUGAR PEAS

8 ounces very small red potatoes
1 pound sugar peas
1 tablespoon butter or margarine
Salt and freshly ground pepper

Cook potatoes, covered, in boiling salted water until tender, about 10 minutes.

Add peas; cover and cook until crisp-tender, about 5 minutes. Drain potatoes and peas.

Add butter; stir to coat with butter. Season with salt and pepper. Serve hot.

Makes 4 to 6 servings.

Variations
If sugar peas aren't available, substitute shelled green peas or snow peas. A pinch of sugar and some finely chopped mint can also be added.

GREEN BEANS & BACON

1 pound fresh green beans
2 bacon slices, minced
1 small white onion, finely chopped
About 1/4 cup water
Salt and freshly ground pepper

Remove ends and any strings from beans. Cut into 1-inch pieces.

Cook bacon in a medium-size saucepan until starting to brown. Add onion; cook until softened. Add green beans and water. Boil, uncovered, 5 minutes.

Reduce heat, cover, and simmer about 10 minutes or until beans are tender. Season with salt and pepper.

Makes about 4 servings.

Variation
Cut 2 yellow squash into quarters and remove seeds. Add to beans after reducing heat.

SOUFFLÉD POTATOES

2 pounds russet potatoes, cut into 1-inch
    cubes
Salt
1/4 cup butter or margarine
1 bunch green onions with tops, finely
    chopped
1/2 cup milk
2 eggs, separated
1 egg white
Freshly ground pepper
Whole green onions (optional) to garnish

Cook potatoes in boiling salted water until
tender, 20 to 30 minutes. Drain potatoes
and mash.

Preheat oven to 400F (205C). Butter a 2-quart
baking dish. Melt butter in a medium-size
skillet. Add green onions; cook until softened. Add onions with butter, the milk, and
egg yolks to potatoes. Beat to combine.

Beat the 3 egg whites until stiff but not dry.
Fold into potato mixture. Spoon into prepared dish. Bake about 30 minutes or until
puffed and top is golden brown. Cut into
squares to serve. Garnish with whole green
onions, if desired.

Makes 4 to 6 servings.

Variation
Sprinkle with 1/2 cup shredded Cheddar cheese
before baking.

BAKED SQUASH

2 small acorn squash
4 tablespoons butter or margarine
1/4 to 1/2 cup packed brown sugar
2 teaspoons ground cinnamon
Freshly grated nutmeg
Salt

Preheat oven to 400F (205C). Cut squash in half crosswise and remove seeds.

Place in a baking pan with a little water and cover tightly. Bake about 45 minutes or until almost tender.

Put 1 tablespoon butter, 1 or 2 tablespoons brown sugar, 1/2 teaspoon cinnamon, and a little nutmeg inside each squash half. Season with salt. Bake, uncovered, until squash is tender. Serve hot. To eat, use your fork to break off bites of the squash and mix with butter mixture.

Makes 4 servings.

TURNIP GREENS & TURNIPS

2 bunches turnip greens
1 pound turnips
2 bacon slices (optional), crisp-cooked,
  crumbled
Salt and freshly ground pepper

Wash greens well to remove all sand. Remove large stems and chop greens.

Peel turnips and cut into 1/2-inch cubes. Combine greens and turnips with 1/3 cup water in a large saucepan. Bring to a boil. Reduce heat, cover and simmer until greens are tender, about 30 minutes. Drain greens; stir in bacon, if using. Season with salt and pepper.

Makes 4 to 6 servings.

CORN PUDDING

3 to 4 ears corn (4 cups kernels)
3 eggs
1 cup milk
1 tablespoon sugar
2 tablespoons butter or margarine,
  melted
Salt and freshly ground white pepper
Bell pepper strips and parsley to garnish

Preheat oven to 350F (175C). Grease a 1-1/2-
quart casserole dish. Cut corn from cobs: first
use a knife to take just the tops off the kernels, then, using the back of the knife, scrape
the remaining corn from the cobs.

Beat eggs until pale yellow. Beat in milk,
sugar, butter, salt, and pepper. Stir in corn.
Pour into prepared dish.

Set casserole dish in a baking pan. Add
enough water to come one-third up side of
dish. Bake about 50 minutes or until a knife
inserted off-center comes out clean. Garnish
with bell pepper and parsley. Serve hot.

Makes 4 to 6 servings.

Note
This is actually a vegetable baked custard. If it
overcooks, it tends to weep.

STIR-FRIED GREENS

**2 bunches kale or collard greens or a
 mixture
2 tablespoons olive oil
1 garlic clove, peeled
Salt and freshly ground pepper**

Rinse greens well in cold water. Shake off
most of the water. Remove large stems from
greens. Cut greens into fine shreds, about
1/8 inch wide.

Heat oil in a wok or large skillet over
medium-high heat. Add garlic clove; cook
until lightly browned and remove.

Add greens to wok. Stir-fry about 5 minutes
or until greens are crisp-tender. Season with
salt and pepper.

Makes 4 servings.

Variation
*Almost any fresh greens can be stir-fried. Tender
greens such as spinach will wilt more and cook
more quickly.*

OAT BATTER BREAD

1 cup low-fat milk
2 tablespoons butter or margarine
2 tablespoons honey
1/2 cup rolled oats
1 (1/4-oz.) package active dry yeast
 (about 1 tablespoon)
1 teaspoon sugar
1/4 cup warm water (110F/45C)
1-1/2 cups whole-wheat flour
1/4 cup oat bran
1 teaspoon salt
About 1-1/4 cups bread flour

Grease a 2-quart casserole dish; set aside. Heat milk, butter, and honey in a small saucepan over medium heat, stirring until butter starts to melt. Pour over oats. Cool to lukewarm.

Dissolve yeast and sugar in warm water in a small bowl. Let stand 5 to 10 minutes or until foamy. Combine yeast mixture and oat mixture with remaining ingredients in a food processor. Process until combined. Mixture will be a stiff batter. Process until smooth and elastic, about 30 seconds.

Place dough in greased casserole dish. Cover with a damp towel. Let rise in a warm place, free from drafts, about 1 hour or until doubled in bulk. Preheat oven to 350F (175C). Bake about 35 minutes or until browned and loaf sounds hollow when tapped on bottom.

Makes 1 loaf, about 10 servings.

REFRIGERATOR POTATO ROLLS

1 (1/4 oz.) package active dry yeast
1/3 cup plus 1 teaspoon sugar
1/4 cup warm water (110F/45C)
3/4 cup potato water
1/2 cup butter or margarine, softened
2 eggs, lightly beaten
1 cup mashed potato (1 large russet
    potato)
1 teaspoon salt
4 to 4-1/2 cups all-purpose flour

Dissolve yeast and sugar in warm water in a large bowl. Let stand 5 to 10 minutes or until foamy. Stir in potato water, butter, eggs, potato, and salt.

Beat in 2 cups of the flour. Stir in enough of the remaining flour to make a moderately stiff dough. Turn out dough onto a floured surface; knead until smooth and elastic. Grease a large bowl. Place dough in bowl; turn to coat. Cover bowl tightly with plastic wrap. Refrigerate up to 24 hours.

Shape dough into rolls as desired. Place on a greased baking sheet. Cover and let rise in a warm place until doubled in bulk, about 1 hour. Preheat oven to 375F (190C). Bake rolls until golden brown. Serve hot.

Makes 18 rolls.

ANGEL BISCUITS

1 teaspoon active dried yeast
1/4 cup lukewarm water (110F, 45C)
2 cups all-purpose flour
1 tablespoon sugar
2 teaspoons baking powder
1/2 teaspoon salt
1/4 teaspoon baking soda
1/4 cup butter or margarine, softened
1/2 cup buttermilk

Preheat oven to 425F (220C). Grease a baking sheet. Dissolve yeast in warm water. Sift flour, sugar, baking powder, salt, and soda into a medium-size bowl.

Stir yeast mixture, butter, and buttermilk into dry ingredients to make a moderately stiff dough. Finish mixing with your hands, if necessary.

Knead dough on a lightly floured board. Roll out dough to about 1/2 inch thick. Cut into rounds with a 2-inch round cutter. Place rounds on greased baking sheet. Bake until raised and golden brown, about 12 minutes. Serve hot.

Makes about 24 biscuits.

Note
These biscuits have the yeasty flavor of rolls with a light biscuit texture.

SOUTHERN BISCUITS

2 cups all-purpose or soft-wheat flour
1 tablespoon baking powder
1/2 teaspoon salt
3 tablespoons vegetable shortening
3 tablespoons butter or margarine,
  chilled
2/3 cup milk

Preheat oven to 450F (225C). Sift flour, baking powder, and salt into a medium-size bowl or bowl of a food processor.

Cut in shortening and butter until mixture resembles coarse crumbs. Stir in enough milk to make a soft dough. Turn out dough onto a lightly floured surface. Knead lightly about 5 times; do not overknead or biscuits will be tough.

Roll out dough to about 1/4 inch thick. Use a 2-inch round cookie cutter to cut dough into rounds. (Reroll dough as needed.) Place on an ungreased baking sheet about 1 inch apart. (Place almost touching for softer biscuits.) Bake 8 to 10 minutes or until puffed and golden brown.

Makes about 18 biscuits.

Variation

Buttermilk Biscuits: Sift 1/2 teaspoon baking soda with dry ingredients and use 2/3 cup buttermilk instead of regular milk. Cut biscuits into 3-inch rounds.

HUSH PUPPIES

1-1/2 cups white cornmeal
1/2 cup all-purpose flour
1 teaspoon baking powder
1 teaspoon salt
About 3/4 cup milk
1 egg, lightly beaten
2 tablespoons vegetable oil
2 green onions with tops, minced
Vegetable oil for cooking

Sift cornmeal, flour, baking powder, and salt into a medium-size bowl. Combine 3/4 cup milk, egg, 2 tablespoons oil, and the green onions in a small bowl.

Stir milk mixture into dry ingredients just until combined. Stir in more milk if mixture is too thick to drop from a spoon.

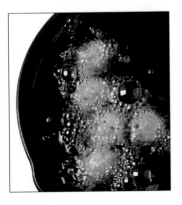

Heat about 2 inches of oil in a heavy pan or deep-fat fryer to 375F (190C). Drop batter into hot oil by spoonfuls. Fry about 3 minutes or until golden brown. Remove with a slotted spoon. Drain on paper towels. Let oil return to temperature before adding the next batch. Serve hot.

Makes about 24 hush puppies.

SPOON BREAD

3/4 cup white cornmeal
1/2 teaspoon salt
2 cups milk
2 tablespoons butter or margarine
1/4 teaspoon white pepper
3 eggs, separated

Preheat oven to 375F (190C). Butter a 1-1/2-quart soufflé dish. Whisk cornmeal and salt into milk in a medium-size heavy saucepan. Cook, stirring constantly, over medium heat until mixture is very thick.

Remove from heat. Stir in butter and white pepper. Let mixture cool slightly. Beat in egg yolks. Beat egg whites in a medium-size bowl until stiff but not dry.

Fold egg whites into cornmeal mixture. Pour into prepared dish. Bake about 35 minutes or until puffed and lightly browned. Serve immediately. (Like a soufflé, spoon bread will fall as it cools.)

Makes about 4 servings.

BUTTERMILK CORNSTICKS

1 cup white cornmeal
1/4 cup all-purpose flour
1 teaspoon baking powder
1/2 teaspoon salt
1/4 teaspoon baking soda
1 cup buttermilk
1 egg, lightly beaten
1 tablespoon vegetable oil

Preheat oven to 450F (225C). Place about 1/2 teaspoon oil into each cornstick form, then place cornstick pan in oven to heat. Sift cornmeal, flour, baking powder, salt, and soda into a medium-size bowl.

Combine buttermilk, egg, and oil in a small bowl. Stir milk mixture into dry ingredients just until combined. Spoon batter into hot cornstick pan. Bake about 10 minutes or until browned on bottom. Serve hot.

Bake in a preheated 8-inch cast-iron skillet about 15 minutes. Recipe can be doubled to make more cornsticks. Reheat cornstick pan and add more oil before baking the second batch.

Makes about 7 cornsticks.

Variation
Buttermilk substitute: Add 1 tablespoon lemon juice or vinegar to a liquid measuring cup. Fill cup with milk. Let stand a few minutes.

FRESH CORNCAKES

2 large ears corn
3/4 cup white cornmeal
1/2 cup all-purpose flour
1 tablespoon baking powder
1/2 teaspoon salt
2 eggs, lightly beaten
3/4 cup milk
2 tablespoons butter or margarine,
  melted

Cut corn from cobs: first use a knife to take just the tops off the kernels, then, using the back of the knife, scrape the remaining corn from the cobs.

Sift cornmeal, flour, baking powder, and salt into a medium-size bowl. Combine corn, eggs, milk, and butter in a small bowl. Stir egg mixture into dry ingredients just until combined.

Heat a nonstick griddle over medium heat. Drop batter by 1/4 cups onto hot griddle. Cook until edges are browned and bubbles form in centers. Turn cakes; cook until cooked through.

Makes about 12 corncakes.

RASPBERRY COFFEECAKE

1-1/4 cups all-purpose flour
2-1/2 teaspoons baking powder
1/4 teaspoon salt
3/4 cup rolled oats
1 tablespoon oat bran
1/2 cup packed light brown sugar
1 egg, lightly beaten
1/4 cup vegetable oil
1-1/4 cups milk
1 teaspoon vanilla extract
1 cup fresh or frozen raspberries,
  thawed if frozen
Crumb Topping:
1/4 cup packed light brown sugar
1/2 cup rolled oats
1/4 cup all-purpose flour
2 tablespoons butter or margarine,
  chilled

Preheat oven to 400F (205C). Butter an 8-inch square pan. Prepare topping: Combine brown sugar, oats, and flour in a small bowl. Cut in butter until crumbly.

Sift flour, baking powder, and salt into a medium-size bowl. Stir in oats, oat bran, and brown sugar. Combine egg, oil, milk, and vanilla in a small bowl. Stir milk mixture into dry ingredients just until moistened. Spoon batter into prepared pan.

Arrange raspberries over batter. Sprinkle raspberries with topping. Bake about 40 minutes or until a wooden pick comes out clean. Cool slightly and cut into squares. Serve warm.

Makes 16 squares.

Orange-Nut Bread

1/2 cup butter or margarine, softened
1/2 cup sugar
2 eggs, lightly beaten
2 cups all-purpose flour
2 teaspoons baking powder
1/2 teaspoon salt
3/4 cup orange juice
1 cup chopped pecans
1 tablespoon grated orange zest

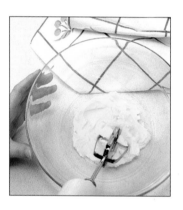

Preheat oven to 325F (165C). Grease a 9″ x 5″ loaf pan. Cream butter and sugar in a medium-size bowl until light and fluffy. Add eggs; beat until thickened.

Sift flour, baking powder, and salt into a medium-size bowl. Beat in flour mixture alternately with orange juice, beginning and ending with flour mixture. Stir in pecans and zest.

Spoon batter into prepared pan. Bake until golden brown and bread springs back when lightly touched in center, about 50 minutes. Remove from pan and cool on a wire rack.

Makes 1 loaf.

PEACH PIE MUFFINS

2 cups all-purpose flour
1/3 cup plus 1 tablespoon sugar
2-1/2 teaspoons baking powder
1/2 teaspoon salt
1-1/4 cups milk
1/4 cup butter or margarine, melted
1 egg, lightly beaten
1 cup chopped firm peaches
  (1 large unpeeled)
1 teaspoon ground cinnamon
1 peach, cut into 12 lengthwise slices

Preheat oven to 400F (205C). Line 12 muffin cups with paper liners or grease cups. Sift flour, 1/3 cup sugar, baking powder, and salt into a medium-size bowl. Combine milk, butter, egg, and chopped peaches in a small bowl.

Stir peach mixture into dry ingredients just until combined. Spoon batter into muffin cups, filling about two-thirds full.

Combine remaining 1 tablespoon sugar and the cinnamon in a small bowl. Dip peach slices in sugar mixture, coating sides of slices with sugar mixture. Place a peach slice in top of each muffin. Bake about 20 minutes or until muffins are browned. Serve warm.

Makes 12 muffins.

Variation
Add 1/2 cup chopped pecans to batter with chopped peaches.

PEANUT BUTTER WAFFLES

2 cups all-purpose flour
2-1/2 tablespoons sugar
1 tablespoon baking powder
1 teaspoon salt
2 cups milk
2 eggs, lightly beaten
**1/4 cup creamy peanut butter, at room
  temperature**
1 teaspoon vanilla extract
1/2 cup chopped peanuts (optional)
Jelly or syrup to serve

Preheat waffle iron. Sift flour, sugar, baking powder, and salt into a medium-size bowl. Combine milk, eggs, peanut butter, and vanilla in a small bowl.

Stir dry ingredients into peanut butter mixture just until combined. Stir in peanuts, if using. (Or sprinkle peanuts on finished waffles.)

Spray waffle iron with nonstick cooking spray. Spoon batter into hot waffle iron and bake according to manufacturer's directions until lightly browned. Serve with syrup.

Makes 4 to 6 waffles.

STRAWBERRY PANCAKES

2 cups all-purpose flour
2 tablespoons granulated sugar
2 teaspoons baking powder
1/2 teaspoon baking soda
1/2 teaspoon salt
1 cup plain low-fat yogurt
1 egg, lightly beaten
3 tablespoons butter or margarine,
    melted
1-1/2 cups of milk
1 cup sliced fresh strawberries
Strawberry syrup, whipped cream, and
    additional strawberries to serve
Mint sprigs to decorate

Preheat a nonstick griddle over medium heat.
Sift flour, sugar, baking powder, soda and salt
into a medium-size bowl. Combine yogurt,
egg, butter, and milk in a small bowl.

Stir yogurt mixture into dry ingredients just
until combined. Stir in strawberries.

Drop batter by 1/4 cups onto preheated griddle. Cook until edges are browned and bubbles form. Turn pancakes; cook until cooked
through. Serve with syrup, whipped cream,
and strawberries. Decorate with mint sprigs.

Makes about 20 (3-inch) pancakes.

PEACH ICE CREAM

1 cup sugar
2 cups peeled, crushed ripe peaches
1 tablespoon fresh lemon juice
1 cup milk
2 cups half-and-half
1 tablespoon vanilla extract
Cookies to serve

Combine sugar, peaches, and lemon juice in a small bowl.

Beat in milk, half-and-half, and vanilla. Refrigerate until chilled.

Pour peach mixture into an ice cream maker. Freeze according to manufacturer's directions. Serve scoops of ice cream with cookies. Transfer any leftovers to freezer containers and freeze up to 1 month. Soften slightly before serving, if needed.

Makes about 1-1/2 quarts.

Note
Use peaches that are completely ripe for the best flavor. Crush peaches with a potato masher or process in a food processor just until chopped.

Peanut Butter Pie

3 cups vanilla ice cream, slightly softened
1 cup creamy peanut butter, room temperature
1 cup marshmallow creme
1 cup chocolate sauce
Crumb Crust:
1-1/2 cups graham cracker crumbs
1/4 cup honey
2 tablespoons butter or margarine, softened

Prepare crust: Combine crumbs, honey, and butter in a medium-size bowl. Press into a 9-inch pie pan. Refrigerate about 30 minutes or until chilled.

Beat ice cream and peanut butter until blended. Stir in marshmallow creme. Do not stir until completely blended. Pour ice cream into chilled pie crust. Cover tightly and freeze at least 4 hours or until firm. The pie can be tightly wrapped and frozen up to 1 month.

Drizzle sauce over pie. Let stand in the refrigerator about 30 minutes to soften slightly before cutting into wedges.

Makes 8 to 10 servings.

LEMON CHESS PIE

1 unbaked 9-inch pie shell
4 eggs, well beaten
1 cup sugar
1/2 cup butter or margarine, softened
1/2 cup lemon juice
1 tablespoon cornmeal
1 tablespoon grated lemon peel
Lemon slices to decorate

Preheat oven to 400F (205C). Cover crust with foil and add dried beans or pie weights. Bake 10 minutes. Remove foil and beans; let cool.

Reduce oven temperature to 325F (165C). Beat eggs, sugar, and butter until light. Beat in lemon juice, cornmeal, and lemon peel.

Pour filling into partially baked shell. Bake about 45 minutes or until a knife inserted off-center comes out clean. Serve warm or chilled. Cut into wedges and decorate with lemon slices. Refrigerate leftovers.

Makes 1 (9-inch) pie.

BLUEBERRY PIE

3/4 cup sugar
3 tablespoons all-purpose flour
4 cups fresh blueberries
Dough for double crust for a 9-inch pie
(page 103)
Vanilla ice cream to serve

Preheat oven to 350F (175C). Combine sugar
and flour in a medium-size bowl. Rinse blueberries and pat dry. Toss blueberries with
sugar mixture; set aside.

Cut dough in half and roll out one half to an
11-inch circle. Use to line a 9-inch pie pan. Fill
pie shell with berry mixture.

Roll out remaining dough to an 11-inch circle. Place over berries. Cut off excess dough.
Crimp edges to seal. Bake about 50 minutes
or until crust is golden brown and the filling
is bubbly and thickened. Serve warm or at
room temperature. Cut into wedges. Serve
with ice cream.

Makes 6 to 8 servings.

BLACKBERRY COBBLER

1 cup sugar
1 tablespoon all-purpose flour
1 tablespoon cornstarch
4 cups fresh or thawed frozen blackberries
Whipping cream, whipped, to serve
Biscuit Crust:
1 cup all-purpose flour
1 teaspoon baking powder
1/4 teaspoon salt
1/4 cup butter or margarine, chilled
6 tablespoons milk

Preheat oven to 425F (220C). Combine the 1
cup sugar, flour, and cornstarch in a small
bowl. Sprinkle over berries in a large bowl;
toss to combine.

Prepare crust: Combine flour, baking powder, and salt in a food processor. Add butter;
process until mixture resembles coarse
crumbs. Add milk; process to make a soft
dough. Knead dough on a lightly floured
board until smooth. Roll out dough to a 12-
inch circle.

Fold dough in half; place fold in center of an
8-inch deep baking dish. Unfold dough in
dish, letting edges drape over rim of pan.
Pour berries into pastry-lined dish. Fold
dough over fruit, pleating to fit. Bake about
30 minutes or until crust is browned and filling is bubbly. Serve warm with whipped
cream.

Makes 6 servings.

COCONUT CREAM PIE

1 cup sugar
2-1/2 tablespoons cornstarch
1 tablespoon all-purpose flour
3 cups milk
3 egg yolks, lightly beaten
1-1/4 cups shredded coconut
1 teaspoon vanilla extract
1 (9-inch) baked pie shell
3 egg whites

Combine 2/3 cup of the sugar, the cornstarch, and flour in a medium-size saucepan. Gradually whisk in milk. Cook, stirring constantly, over medium heat until mixture comes to a boil. Boil 2 minutes, stirring constantly.

Remove from heat. Whisk 1/2 cup of hot mixture into beaten egg yolks. Whisk egg mixture into hot mixture. Cook, stirring constantly, about 2 minutes or until thickened. Pour mixture into a heatproof bowl. Stir in 1 cup of the coconut and the vanilla. Cool slightly, stirring occasionally. Pour into pie shell. Preheat oven to 350F (175C).

Beat egg whites in a medium-size bowl until soft peaks form. Gradually beat in the remaining 1/3 cup sugar until peaks are stiff and glossy. Spread meringue over warm filling in swirls. Sprinkle with remaining 1/4 cup coconut. Bake about 5 minutes or until meringue is golden. Cool and cut into wedges. Refrigerate leftovers.

Makes about 6 servings.

PECAN PIE

3 eggs
1 cup sugar
1 cup dark corn syrup
1/4 cup butter or margarine, melted
1 teaspoon vanilla extract
2 cups pecan halves
Crust:
1-1/2 cups all-purpose flour
1/2 teaspoon salt
1/4 cup butter or margarine, chilled
1/4 cup solid vegetable shortening
About 4 tablespoons cold water

Preheat oven to 350F (175C). Prepare crust: Combine flour and salt in a medium-size bowl. Cut in butter until particles are the size of peas. Cut in shortening until mixture resembles bread crumbs. Add water a little at a time, mixing with a fork until mixture just holds together. Form dough into a ball; refrigerate 30 minutes.

Roll out dough on a lightly floured surface to an 11-inch circle. Fit dough into a 9-inch pie pan. Trim edges and flute, if desired. Beat eggs until light in a medium-size bowl. Stir in sugar, corn syrup, butter, and vanilla. Gently stir in pecans.

Pour mixture into pie shell. Bake about 55 minutes or until filling is firm and pecans are browned. Serve warm.

Makes 1 (9-inch) pie, about 6 servings.

Note
Crust for a double-crust pie: Double recipe. Cut dough in half before rolling.

Glazed Strawberry Pie

1 quart fresh strawberries
1/2 cup red currant jelly
1 tablespoon cornstarch
Red food coloring (optional)
1 (9-inch) baked pie shell
1/2 cup whipping cream
2 tablespoons powdered sugar
1 teaspoon vanilla extract

Rinse berries and remove caps. Reserve about 3-1/2 cups of the most perfect berries for the pie. Mash remaining berries. Combine mashed berries, jelly, and cornstarch in a medium-size saucepan. Cook, stirring, over medium heat until mixture is bubbly and thickened. Cool slightly; stir in food coloring, if using.

Spoon some of the cooked mixture into bottom of pie shell. Arrange berries in pie shell. Spoon remaining glaze over berries. Refrigerate until set.

Whip cream in a small bowl until soft peaks form. Beat in powdered sugar and vanilla. Serve whipped cream with pie.

Makes 1 (9-inch) pie.

SWEET POTATO PIE

1 cup mashed sweet potatoes
1/2 cup packed light brown sugar
2 eggs, lightly beaten
2 tablespoons butter or margarine,
   softened
1 tablespoon all-purpose flour
1/2 teaspoon ground cinnamon
1/4 teaspoon ground cloves
1/8 teaspoon freshly grated nutmeg
Dash of salt
1/2 cup milk
1 (9-inch) unbaked pie shell
Vanilla ice cream to serve
Nut Topping:
1/4 cup packed light brown sugar
1/2 cup chopped pecans or walnuts

Preheat oven to 375F (190C). Combine sweet potatoes, sugar, eggs, butter, flour, spices, and salt in a medium-size bowl.

Stir in milk. Pour into pie shell. Bake about 30 minutes or until filling is set. Remove pie from oven. Prepare topping: Combine sugar and nuts in a small bowl. Preheat broiler.

Cover crust with foil. Sprinkle topping over filling. Broil until sugar melts and caramelizes. Do not burn. Serve warm with ice cream or refrigerate and serve chilled. Refrigerate leftovers.

Makes 6 to 8 servings.

Hint
One (12-oz.) sweet potato can be cooked in a microwave oven until soft, then peeled and mashed for this recipe.

Angel Pie with Lemon Curd

4 egg whites
1/4 teaspoon salt
1/4 teaspoon cream of tartar
1 cup sugar
1 cup whipping cream
Lemon slices and lemon leaves (optional)
    to decorate
Lemon Curd:
1/2 cup sugar
3 egg yolks
2 tablespoons butter or margarine
6 tablespoons lemon juice
Grated peel of 1 lemon

Preheat oven to 275F (135C). Butter and flour a 9-inch pie pan. Beat egg whites, salt, and cream of tartar in a medium-size bowl until soft peaks form. Gradually beat in sugar; beat until stiff and glossy. Spread beaten egg whites in prepared pan, mounding the edges. Bake about 1 hour or until firm and set.

Prepare curd: Combine all ingredients in a medium-size stainless steel bowl that will fit in a saucepan. Cook, stirring occasionally, over simmering water until mixture thickens, about 15 minutes. Cool curd.

Beat cream until stiff. Spread two-thirds of cream over meringue shell, then spread cooled curd over cream. Spoon remaining cream into a pastry bag fitted with a star tip. Pipe cream around edge of pie. Decorate with lemon slices and lemon leaves. Refrigerate up to 4 hours before serving. (If kept too long after filling, the meringue will soften.)

Makes about 8 servings.

KENTUCKY APPLE STACK CAKE

2 cups all-purpose flour
2 teaspoons baking powder
1/4 teaspoon baking soda
1/4 cup packed light brown sugar
1/4 cup granulated sugar
1/3 cup butter or margarine, chilled
1 egg, lightly beaten
About 1/2 cup buttermilk
1/2 teaspoon vanilla extract
Powdered sugar
Spicy Apple Filling:
2 cups dried apples (8 oz.), chopped
1/2 cup packed light brown sugar
1-1/2 teaspoons ground cinnamon
1/4 teaspoon each ground cloves
   and allspice

Preheat oven to 425F (220C). Grease 2 baking sheets. Combine flour, baking powder, soda, and sugar in a food processor. Add butter; process until mixture resembles coarse crumbs. Add egg, buttermilk, and vanilla; process to form a soft dough. Shape dough into a ball. Divide dough into 3 equal pieces. Pat each piece into a 9-inch circle. Place on baking sheets. Bake about 15 minutes or until centers spring back when lightly pressed. Remove from pans; cool on wire racks. Prepare filling: Combine apples and enough water to cover in a large saucepan. Cook, stirring occasionally, over medium heat about 30 minutes or until apples are soft and water is absorbed. Add more water if needed and stir apples more frequently near end of cooking time.

Mash apples. Stir in brown sugar and spices; cool. Place one cake layer on a serving plate. Top with one-half of apples. Top with another cake layer and remaining apples, then remaining cake layer. Wrap in plastic wrap and let stand overnight before serving. Sprinkle top with powdered sugar; cut into wedges.

Makes 8 servings.

WHITE COCONUT CAKE

3 cups sifted cake flour
1 tablespoon baking powder
1/2 teaspoon salt
1/2 cup vegetable shortening
1/4 cup butter or margarine, softened
1 cup sugar
1 teaspoon vanilla extract
1 cup milk
4 egg whites
Lemon Curd (page 106), made with lime juice and peel
1 cup shredded coconut
Fluffy Frosting:
1-1/2 cups sugar
2 egg whites
5 tablespoons water
1 teaspoon vanilla extract
1/4 teaspoon cream of tartar

Preheat oven to 350F (175C). Grease and flour 2 (9-inch) round cake pans and line bottoms with waxed paper. Sift flour, baking powder, and salt into a small bowl.

Cream shortening, butter, and sugar until light and fluffy. Beat in vanilla. Add dry ingredients to creamed mixture alternately with milk, beginning and ending with dry ingredients. Beat after each addition.

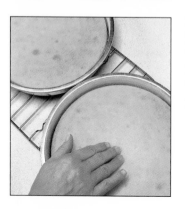

Beat egg whites in a medium-size bowl until stiff but not dry. Fold egg whites into batter. Pour batter into prepared pans. Bake about 30 minutes or until cakes spring back when pressed in center. Cool in pans 10 minutes. Turn out onto a wire rack, remove waxed paper, and let cool completely.

Cut each cake layer into 2 horizontal layers.
Place one layer on a cake plate. Top with
about one-third of the curd, then with
another cake layer. Repeat with remaining
curd and cake layers, ending with a cake layer.

Prepare frosting: Combine all frosting ingredients in the top of a double boiler or a stainless steel bowl. Cook, beating constantly, over
simmering water until frosting is fluffy and
forms soft peaks, about 7 minutes.

Spread frosting over top and side of cake.
Sprinkle coconut over frosting and press
lightly with your fingers.

Makes 1 (9-inch) cake, about 10 servings.

JAM CAKE

2 cups all-purpose flour
2 teaspoons baking powder
1/2 teaspoon baking soda
1/2 teaspoon salt
1 teaspoon ground cinnamon
1 teaspoon ground allspice
1/2 cup vegetable shortening
1 cup sugar
2 eggs
1 cup blackberry or strawberry jam
1/2 cup buttermilk
Powdered sugar
Fresh strawberries, mint, and whipped
cream (optional) to serve

Preheat oven to 350F (175C). Grease and flour a 9-inch tube pan. Sift flour, baking powder, soda, salt, cinnamon, and allspice into a small bowl.

Cream shortening and sugar together until light and fluffy. Beat in eggs, one at a time, until pale yellow. Beat in jam.

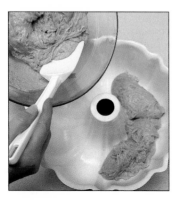

Add dry ingredients to creamed mixture alternately with buttermilk, beginning and ending with dry ingredients. Beat after each addition. Pour batter into prepared pan. Bake about 45 minutes or until a wooden pick inserted in center of cake comes out clean. Cool in pan 10 minutes. Turn out onto a wire rack and cool completely. Sift powdered sugar over cake. Fill center of cake with strawberries and mint leaves. Cut into slices to serve; serve with the strawberries and whipped cream, if desired.

Makes 1 (9-inch) cake, about 10 servings.

CHOCOLATE BREAD PUDDING

3 cups 1-inch cubes of day-old cinnamon
   rolls
1/2 cup coarsely chopped pecans,
   toasted
1/3 cup sugar
1/4 cup unsweetened cocoa powder
3 eggs, lightly beaten
3 cups milk
2 teaspoons vanilla extract
Vanilla Sauce:
1 cup sugar
2 tablespoons cornstarch
2 tablespoons all-purpose flour
4 cups milk
2 eggs, well beaten
1 tablespoon vanilla extract

Butter a 2-quart baking dish. Combine rolls
and pecans in buttered dish.

Combine sugar and cocoa in a medium-size
bowl. Beat in eggs until foamy. Gradually beat
in milk and vanilla. Pour over roll mixture.
Let stand about 30 minutes to soften rolls.
Preheat oven to 350F (175C). Bake pudding
about 50 minutes or until a knife inserted
off-center comes out clean.

Prepare sauce: Combine sugar, cornstarch,
and flour in a large saucepan. Gradually
whisk in milk. Cook, stirring, over medium
heat until mixture comes to a boil. Remove
from heat. Stir 1 cup of hot mixture into
eggs; return to heat. Cook, stirring, 2 minutes. Cool; stir in vanilla. Serve pudding
warm or at room temperature with sauce.
Refrigerate leftovers.

Makes 6 servings.

PECAN PRALINES

2 cups packed light brown sugar
1 cup granulated sugar
1 cup half-and-half
1/4 cup butter or margarine
2 tablespoons light corn syrup
2 teaspoons vanilla extract
2 cups coarsely chopped pecans

Combine sugars, half-and-half, butter, and corn syrup in a large heavy saucepan. Cook, stirring constantly, over medium heat until sugars are dissolved and mixture comes to a boil. Wash down any sugar crystals with a pastry brush that has been dipped in water.

Add a candy thermometer, if using. Cook, stirring occasionally, until mixture reaches the soft-ball stage (a soft ball forms when a teaspoon of mixture is dropped into a cup of cold water) or 238F (115C). Pour into a heat-proof bowl and cool to lukewarm (110F, 45C). Meanwhile, line 2 large baking sheets with waxed paper.

Add vanilla and beat with a wooden spoon or heavy-duty mixer until thickened and no longer glossy. Beat in pecans. Drop by spoonfuls onto waxed paper and spread into patties. (If candy sets up before all patties are formed, stir in hot water a teaspoon at a time.) Let cool completely.

Makes about 50 candies.

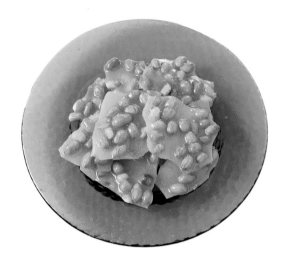

TRADITIONAL PEANUT BRITTLE

2 cups sugar
1 cup light corn syrup
1 cup water
1/4 teaspoon cream of tartar
2 cups shelled raw peanuts
2 tablespoons butter or margarine
1/2 teaspoon baking soda

Butter 2 baking sheets. Set aside. Combine sugar, corn syrup, water, and cream of tartar in a heavy medium-size saucepan. Cook, stirring constantly, over medium heat until sugar is dissolved and mixture comes to a boil. Wash down any sugar crystals with a pastry brush that has been dipped in water.

Add candy thermometer. Cook, stirring occasionally, until mixture reaches the soft-ball stage. Add peanuts. Cook until mixture reaches the hard-crack stage (mixture separates into hard threads when dropped into cold water) or 300F (150C).

Remove from heat. Stir in butter and soda; immediately pour onto buttered baking sheets. Using 2 forks, stretch as thinly as possible. Cool and break into small pieces. Store candy in an airtight container.

Makes about 2 pounds.

MINT JULEP

1/2 cup sugar
1/2 cup water
2 large mint sprigs plus extra for decoration
Crushed ice
3 ounces bourbon

Add sugar and water to a small saucepan. Cook, stirring, until sugar dissolves. Bring to a boil. Cool syrup.

Add 1/4 cup syrup to a 10-ounce glass. Add 1 mint sprig and muddle (crush) mint with syrup. Discard mint.

Fill glass with crushed ice. Add 1-1/2 ounces bourbon. Stir and add a fresh mint sprig Repeat with remaining ingredients.

Makes 2 drinks.

METRIC CHARTS

Comparison to Metric Measure				
When You Know	Symbol	Multiply By	To Find	Symbol
teaspoons	tsp	5.0	milliliters	ml
tablespoons	tbsp	15.0	milliliters	ml
fluid ounces	fl. oz.	30.0	milliters	ml
cups	c	.24	liters	l
pints	pt.	.047	liters	l
quarts	qt.	.095	liters	l
ounces	oz.	28.0	grams	g
pounds	lb.	0.45	kilograms	kg
Fahrenheit	F	5/9 (after subtracting 32)	Celsius	C

Fahrenheit to Celsius

F	C
200–205	95
220–225	105
245–250	120
275	135
300–305	150
325–330	175
345–350	175
370–375	190
400–405	205
425–430	220
445–450	230
470–475	245
500	260

Liquid Measure to Milliliters

¼ teaspoon	=	1.25 milliliters
½ teaspoon	=	2.5 milliliters
¾ teaspoon	=	3.75 milliliters
1 teaspoon	=	5.0 milliliters
1¼ teaspoon	=	6.25 milliliters
1½ teaspoon	=	7.5 milliliters
1¾ teaspoon	=	8.75 milliliters
2 teaspoon	=	10.0 milliters
1 tablespoon	=	15.0 milliliters
2 tablespoon	=	30.0 milliliters

Liquid Measure to Liters

¼ cup	=	0.06 liters
½ cup	=	0.12 liters
¾ cup	=	0.18 liters
1 cup	=	0.24 liters
1¼ cups	=	.3 liters
1½ cups	=	0.36 liters
2 cups	=	0.48 liters
2½ cups	=	0.6 liters
3 cups	=	0.72 liters
3½ cups	=	0.84 liters
4 cups	=	0.96 liters
4½ cups	=	1.08 liters
5 cups	=	1.2 liters
5½ cups	=	1.32 liters

INDEX

I N D E X

INDEX